SPEAK-UP
CULTURE

When Leaders Truly Listen,

People Step Up

SPEAK-UP

STEPHEN SHEDLETZKY

CULTURE

● ● PAGE TWO

Cataloguing in publication information is available from Library and Archives Canada.
ISBN 978-1-77458-284-8 (paperback)
ISBN 978-1-77458-285-5 (ebook)

Page Two
pagetwo.com

Edited by Kendra Ward
Copyedited by Steph VanderMeulen
Proofread by Alison Strobel
Cover design by Peter Cocking
Interior design and illustrations by Fiona Lee
Indexed by Stephen Ullstrom
Printed and bound in Canada by Friesens
Distributed in Canada by Raincoast Books
Distributed in the US and internationally by Macmillan

23 24 25 26 27   5 4 3 2 1

SpeakUpCulture.com

*For the leaders who have taught and
shown me the power of a speak-up culture.*

*And for Julie . . . who makes
it safe and worth it to speak up.*

---

*"Leaders who do not listen will
eventually be surrounded by
people who have nothing to say."*
ANDY STANLEY

Contents

What's at Stake?

OCTOBER 29, 2018, began like any other day for the fishermen who set out to trawl for prawns in the Java Sea, off the north coast of Indonesia's Karawang Regency. From the deck of their teak boats, they watched the sun rise, the water still as glass. But at 6:32 a.m., the quiet of the morning came to a piercing halt. A passenger airplane dropped from the sky, nose-first. A sound louder than thunder filled the air as the aircraft collided with the sea, sending shockwaves through the water.

Lion Air Flight 610, a new Boeing 737 MAX, had crashed.

The flight—from Jakarta to Pangkal Pinang—was meant to be an hour long, but just two minutes after takeoff, the pilots were alerted to issues with altitude and airspeed. Lights blinked, bells rang, and the controls shook. The pilots attempted to adjust, but the airliner seemed to fight them, dropping toward the water every time they lifted the nose skyward. They lost control of the plane as it dove nose-first.

Just twelve minutes after it took off, the 737 MAX hit the water at five hundred miles per hour, killing all 189 people on board. People traveling for work and pleasure—parents and spouses, children and siblings. All gone.

A brand-new, state-of-the-art airplane should not fall out of a perfect-weather sky.

Was this disaster an isolated incident or was there something larger transpiring?

THE ORIGINAL Boeing 737, a short-haul commercial aircraft, first flew in 1967. It was so popular, it became the Honda Accord of the sky—a ubiquitous, go-to aircraft for virtually every major airline, from Aeroméxico to United. In fact, every one and a half seconds, a Boeing 737 takes off somewhere in the world.

The 737 MAX was Boeing's latest iteration of its bestselling airplane. It served as a significant upgrade to the previous design, doubling the original 737's thrust while significantly reducing fuel consumption. When the MAX was introduced in 2016, record-breaking orders poured in. It was an exciting time for Boeing, the largest aerospace company in the world, responsible for the safe transport of millions of people. While executives and investors must have been pleased with the record climb of its stock price, the employees tasked with manufacturing the new plane were scrambling to keep up.

Demands to make more planes and move quicker than ever before, with seemingly little regard for those doing the work, left much room for error. It was a combination of errors and leadership oversights that proved catastrophic.

Part of Boeing's sales promise for the MAX was a far improved and upgraded 737 that required very little retraining for pilots—a great, low-cost proposition for airlines. But the MAX was a significantly different plane, which should have required airlines to conduct substantial pilot training.

Much larger engines on the 737 MAX changed the aerodynamics of the plane in a less desirable way. To compensate, Boeing engineered a powerful software system called the Maneuvering Characteristics Augmentation System (MCAS), which performed a safety-critical function to help the plane avoid a stall. To work properly, it needed accurate airflow data, which came from sensors located on the front of the plane. The MAX had two such sensors. The MCAS, however, gained airflow data from only one of them. This meant it had a single point of failure—no backup should it fail.

Investigations revealed that in the case of Lion Air Flight 610, this sensor had indeed failed. The MCAS essentially overrode the pilots' corrections in response to the sensor's misinformation. The pilots were seemingly fighting against a possessed airplane.

How were these planes deemed fit to fly?

Boeing chalked the crash up to issues with the airline, specifically inexperienced foreign pilots who lacked sufficient training, a narrative that seemed to fit given that Lion Air had previous problems with safety. An even greater and wicked irony is that, in June 2017, Lion Air had asked Boeing for additional simulator training. Boeing persuaded Lion Air out of this request. On November 13, 2018, former Boeing CEO Dennis Muilenburg shared in a Fox Business interview that the now deceased pilots had possessed "the ability to handle" the mechanical issues they had experienced onboard the MAX, and asserted, "We provide all the information that's needed to safely fly our airplanes." In truth, in the over 1,600-page flight manual of Boeing's 737 MAX at that time, the aircraft's new MCAS computer system was mentioned only once by name—in the glossary of abbreviated terms.

Seventeen weeks later, on March 10, 2019, another new 737 MAX—Ethiopian Airlines Flight 302—crashed six minutes after takeoff, mirroring the same issue and killing 157 more people.

Had Boeing's leaders cultivated a different type of work culture—a speak-up culture—and made it a priority to listen and act, perhaps both of these tragedies could have been prevented.

ONE BOEING employee, among others, was consistently and courageously vocal about the production issues and potential

What if the risk to speak up were **both safe and worth it?**

dangers leading up to and beyond the first 737 MAX crash. Ed Pierson, a retired US naval officer, started working for Boeing at its Renton factory near Seattle, Washington, in 2008 and became a senior manager in 2015. In his final role with the company, he oversaw production support for the 737 final assembly. In the fourth quarter of 2017, he became increasingly troubled by a multitude of issues occurring at the plant. According to Pierson, there were chronic shortages of parts and of test equipment for legally required testing. With orders pouring in and production backlogs building up, the factory even ran out of space to park unfinished airplanes, so they started parking them in the employee parking lots.

The people working the production line were trying to keep up with the thousands of 737 MAX airplanes on order. They were exhausted from putting in long hours to meet demand, and pressure was only increasing. When frontline staff inevitably ran behind, project status meetings turned into large, tension-filled town hall meetings, sometimes gathering a hundred or more workers. Some employees reported feeling publicly shamed and bullied by senior leaders for falling behind. "It [sent] a very clear and chilling message to people," Pierson commented.

Fearing for the safety of Boeing's aircraft and the people who would be on them, Pierson shared his concerns in June 2018 with the general manager of the 737 production line, a senior executive. Quoted in *Corporate Crime Reporter* during an interview, Pierson wrote in an email, "'Frankly right now, all of my internal warning bells are going off. For the first time in my life, I'm sorry to say that I'm hesitant about putting my family on a Boeing airplane.'" But Pierson felt ignored.

Discouraged and worried he'd be fired, Pierson nevertheless pressed on. He insisted on meeting face-to-face with the general manager and in that meeting recommended that Boeing shut down production until the issues could be addressed. The senior executive said it couldn't be done. Pierson told the general manager that he'd seen operations in the military shut down for far less. The general manager responded, "'The military is not a profit-making organization.'"

Pierson pushed back, "'What do you mean? You are the head person. You are in charge of 8,000 people here. Between you and the CEO there are like two people.'"

In the *Corporate Crime Reporter* interview, Pierson explained, "'Prior to this meeting, I had high regard for [the general manager] ... I think he was under a huge amount of pressure [from his superiors at the Boeing corporate offices] to get airplanes out the door. We had sales goals and delivery goals. He was the person who could have stopped the line. Let's slow down, let's get our act together, let our suppliers catch up, let our people get some rest.'"

Although Pierson intended to work at Boeing for another five years, after witnessing the chaos on the factory floor and top management seemingly ignoring his and others' warnings on production quality issues, he chose to retire in August 2018. But his work was far from done.

Two months later, Lion Air 610 crashed. Pierson was an assistant high school football coach at the time. "'I was in my living room putting the scouting report together for the next team we were going to play,'" he said. "'And the news flash came up. And it said—737 *crashes into the ocean*. And it was horrifying.'" In the weeks that followed, Pierson continued to follow the news and preliminary investigations keenly. He sprang into action.

In December 2018, Pierson requested that Boeing's CEO investigate the Renton factory, where the 737 MAX was produced, and call in international accident investigators. Once again, he was ignored. Over the next three months, he appealed to the company's chief counsel and board of directors, to no avail. He was determined to prevent the tragedy of another plane going down.

In March 2019, when Ethiopian Airlines Flight 302 crashed after a nearly identical struggle between the pilots and the plane's MCAS software, Pierson raised his concerns again, this time with the National Transportation Safety Board (NTSB), a government investigative agency. It too declined to act, sending him a letter that read that the "concerns fall outside the scope of the NTSB's role in the 737 MAX accident investigations." When Pierson reached out to the Federal Aviation Administration (FAA), he was told that the NTSB was indeed the proper party to handle such information—yet another dead end.

Eventually, Ed Pierson became a whistleblower, going public in December 2019 and testifying before the US Congress. Ultimately, he got his message across, but it took years, his early resignation, two planes, and 346 lives lost before the right people would listen and act. Pierson continues to be a safety advocate, determined to do everything in his power to do right by the families who lost loved ones, and the public.

AT ITS most innocuous, not having a speak-up culture leads to missed opportunities, and at its most severe, an organization can crumble, or devastation can be the result. Although the dramatic case of the 737 MAX is one of many examples highlighted in the text ahead, it creates cause for questions, both in the case of Boeing and for leadership and organizational culture at large.

How different would things be if leaders prioritized people over profits? What if leaders primarily showed commitment to the people they serve—in the case of Boeing, the employees, airlines, flight crew, and passengers? What might happen if senior executives valued the input bravely and rightfully provided by employees? What would be different if leaders cultivated a speak-up culture—an environment marked by psychological safety and perceived impact? A belief that the risk to speak up were both safe and worth it.

How Did This Happen?

"We need to stop just pulling people out of the river. We need to go upstream and find out why they're falling in."

DESMOND TUTU

CREATING A speak-up culture isn't crucial only for airplane manufacturers, militaries, or medical professions—where the results of a failure are clearly life and death. Dr. Casey Chosewood at the National Institute for Occupational Safety and Health found that our relationship with our boss has a greater effect on our health than our relationship with our family doctor. Leaders at every level of an organization ought to feel the full weight of the privilege, responsibility, and obligation that such a relationship holds. Leaders are responsible not only for people's livelihoods but also for their well-being. Leadership in and of itself—in all industries—is a life-feeding or life-depleting line of work. Proceed with caution and care.

Former Boeing CEO Dennis Muilenburg had a good reputation. As Jeffrey Sonnenfeld, author and senior associate dean for leadership studies at the Yale School of Management, describes, before the MAX devastation, Muilenburg was known as "a smart, honest, humble, well-regarded engineer"; he had been with Boeing throughout his thirty-five-year career. Although this would far from excuse anyone for a disastrous corporate scandal, it does suggest that seemingly *good* people are capable of unintentionally doing wrong, harmful, and even fatal things. Countless examples and studies prove this point. Look no further than Stanley Milgram's well-known experiment on obedience to authority—where many participants obeyed an authority figure even when they believed they were harming someone.

Might any of us have behaved the same way if we had been in the same situation?

Of course, creating a speak-up culture is no guarantee. It takes deliberate and intentional work to create, maintain, and scale.

What's a Speak-Up Culture, Anyway?

Before we go any further, let's set a definition. A speak-up culture is an environment in which people feel it is both *safe* and *worth it* to share their

- **ideas** (even if they're half-baked),
- **concerns** (even if they're unpopular and/or personal),
- **disagreements** (especially with senior leaders), and
- **mistakes** (believing it will lead to improvements, not punishments).

I have had experiences in my career of being a part of speak-up cultures, and they were marvelous. I hope you have too! The breadth and depth of what you can discuss with colleagues, the relationships and friendships that can form, and the benefit to the organization in the form of trust, cooperation, collaboration, creativity, and innovation are all good for business and people. I have also been on teams, involved with organizations, and in relationships that are far more toxic, spending inordinate amounts of time and energy walking on eggshells and avoiding leaders, not wishing to step on a landmine that may be in the next meeting, email, or conversation. Such cultures are bad for business and for people's mental and physical well-being. We have seen the results of this from decades' worth of workforce engagement scores, not to mention what's unfolded with the Great Resignation, quiet quitting, and whatever other turns of phrase are born from organizational cultures and behaviors that make people's work-life experience worse. It's time for change. We all deserve better.

This book is written for leaders, not necessarily by title or authority but by behavior. It is for senior leaders who believe in a leadership and business philosophy that puts people ahead of profits, a great irony being that organizations with such a culture outperform their cutthroat, performance-focused counterparts time and again. If you need proof, one study found that trustworthy companies outperform low-trust companies by 2.5 times.

This book is also for managers and leaders in the middle. Perhaps they have had some good, maybe even great, as well as not-so-great leaders before them as examples. They wish to lead in a better way and cultivate the types of work environments that people want to show up to, physically or virtually, every day. While these leaders certainly feel the tensions, pressures, and realities of operating an organization, they know there is a better way, and they wish to lead that charge.

Finally, this book is for aspiring leaders—those who may not yet hold a title or position of leadership but are already committed to behaving as a leader.

While this vision of organizational culture and leadership is appealing, it's not easy to achieve, and we're not there yet. Indeed, we may never get there completely. Sound leadership and healthy speak-up cultures are infinite games—there is no arrival. There is only the journey. There is always more work, more improvement, and more development—of us and others—to be done. Much needs to be done globally, in all industries—from education to politics, government to law enforcement, military to for-profit, social causes and beyond—for healthy speak-up cultures to become the norm.

The Good Samaritan

The only real requisite of leadership is followers—people who willingly go in the direction you're going because they believe in you, they trust you, and they want to be a part of where you're headed. Leadership does not live in a title. It lives in behavior.

We can bring this point to life with a story revealing where we get the term "good Samaritan." It comes from, of all places, the Bible.

Luke 10:29–37 can help us explore the effects of pressure on ethics. This passage tells the story of a man who was traveling from Jerusalem to Jericho when he was accosted by robbers. They stole his clothes, beat him up, and left him for dead. A priest and a Levite walking the same route both passed him by—not what you'd expect from such devout individuals. Ultimately, a third man, hailing from Samaria, stopped to help the stranger in need, cleaned his wounds, and brought him to a nearby inn to heal.

The passage asks, "Which of these three do you think was a neighbor to the man who fell into the hands of robbers?" In other words, who is the virtuous one? Who is the leader?

The answer?

"The one who had mercy on him." The one who stopped to help.

So, why did the priest and the Levite, seemingly ethical people, fail to help the man on the side of the road?

In the early 1970s, social psychologists John Darley and Daniel Batson set out to answer that question by putting the biblical passage to the test, quite literally, conducting an experiment called the "Good Samaritan Study." They told Princeton Theological Seminary students that they were participating in a study on religious education. When the seminary students arrived for the study, they were sent to another building, where they would give a talk. On the way to the second location, each participant encountered a man on the ground who moaned and coughed, obviously in need of help. The researchers then graded participants' behavior, from not even noticing the victim to stopping to ask if the man needed help and making sure he got it.

The researchers found that one variable influenced the participants' behavior above all else—time pressure. Before they left for the talk, one group of participants was told they had a few minutes until they were scheduled to speak (low hurry), one group was told the talk would begin right then (medium hurry), and the final group was told they were late (high hurry). Of those in a low-hurry situation, 63 percent stopped to help; 45 percent of those in medium-hurry situations helped; and only 10 percent of those in high-hurry situations helped. In some instances, participants even stepped over the stranger in need!

Personally, I feel that even 63 percent is low. What better excuse is there to be late to give a talk on the good Samaritan and being a virtuous person than "I'm sorry I'm late, I had to help a stranger in need"?

In the end, the researchers concluded that:

- ethics could become a luxury as the speed of our lives increases, and

- time pressure may have affected participants' cognition, inhibiting their ability to immediately recognize an emergency when they saw one.

Some of the participants who didn't stop explained that they felt conflicted between helping the man and serving the experimenter. Thus, their decisions weren't necessarily because of the quality of their character but were influenced by the pressure they felt to perform their assigned task.

At Boeing, the impact of external and internal pressure on culture and behavior was visible across the organization, cascading from as high up as the company's executives and board of directors down to their high-level supervisors, and seemingly to operators on the factory floor. Safety and ethics evidently fell by the wayside because of aggressive and sometimes unrealistic deadlines, financial targets and the expectations of investors and Wall Street analysts, big purchasers like Southwest Airlines pressuring Boeing to eliminate costly pilot training, and an extremely competitive market landscape with counterpart Airbus. Boeing leaders were making hurried decisions resulting in the prioritization of sales and revenues over technical and safety requirements. Even when people—like senior manager Ed Pierson—spoke up, raising concerns to the right people, they apparently weren't heard. Not until the second plane, Ethiopian Airlines Flight 302, crashed did the president of the United States intervene, ordering the grounding of the 737 MAX. The FAA and Boeing were finally forced to address the safety issues.

In a speak-up culture, people feel it is both safe and worth it **to share ideas, concerns, disagreements, and mistakes.**

But We're Good People, Aren't We?

To understand more about how some leaders might rationalize the pressure they place on others and themselves, we can look to the concept of ethical fading, coined by researchers Ann Tenbrunsel and David Messick. Ethical fading occurs when we are so focused on other aspects of a decision that its ethical dimensions disappear from view. It is a form of self-deception that occurs subconsciously and allows us to behave in immoral ways while maintaining the conviction that we are good, moral people. We unwittingly avoid the moral component of a decision so that we can do or get what we want *and* continue to believe that we are good people.

When we look back on the choices we made in service of that want, we rationalize them to align with our (often flawed) moral conception of ourselves. Ethical fading is one reason many of us experience a disparity between how we *want* to behave and how we actually behave.

Tenbrunsel described the dangers of ethical fading in another transportation-based catastrophe. In the early 1970s, Ford found issues with its new Pinto model. During crash tests, the car's gas tank would often explode—a defect that could cause injury or death. When the company crunched the numbers, however, it found that settling lawsuits would be cheaper than fixing the problem right away (which would have cost, per car, about US$(1978)10 to $15). To avoid the ethical implications of such a choice, Ford executives framed it as a "smart business decision." It took seven years, at least twenty-seven confirmed deaths and nine hundred injuries, and a national investigation for Ford to recall the vehicles. It also cost the company US$(1978)20 million in recalled vehicles and $128 million in a single civil suit alone—of the one hundred-plus lawsuits filed.

Tenbrunsel and Messick explain that euphemisms and jargon are one way people obscure the ethics of their decisions to the outside world, and to themselves: "We engage in 'aggressive' accounting practices, not illegal ones. There may be some 'externalities' associated with a strategy, not harmful to others or the environment. We have 'collateral damage' in military campaigns, not civilian deaths."

With both ethical fading and the impact of pressure on our ethics and decision-making, what steps can we take to combat both? The answer, in both cases, is leadership.

Mind the Say-Do Gap

Many leaders set out to start and grow an organization with the best intentions. They want to build an operation that provides immense value, not just for financial stakeholders but also for employees, customers, and society alike. Over time, though, external and internal pressures can increase the gap between what leaders say and what they do.

Of course, everyone is entitled to run their organization as they wish. If you've built a profit-first operation and you're transparent about it, I can accept that. It's honest, and it enables prospective and current employees and customers alike to make informed choices about where they work and buy from. Issues arise, however, when organizations make bold statements about their culture, products, and services and don't take genuine steps to fulfill them.

Too many leaders and organizations say they stand for creating social good while proliferating toxic internal cultures and unethical practices. Before we try to "change the world," let's work on bettering the experience of the people we're depending on to do it.

"The road to hell is paved with good intentions" is an adage for a reason: the only way to identify someone's values is through their behavior. In other words, what matters most is what we do.

As a leader, you must focus not only on what you do but also on what you can control. Managing what is within your control—like behaviors, processes, and policies—leads to your outcomes. You can get into trouble when you prioritize results—like revenue or performance—because you don't have control over these. That's like incentivizing someone to achieve a goal they have little or no influence over.

Here's a great example of what can happen when leaders focus on what they can control. A colleague of mine went over and above during her employer's busiest time of the year. She worked in a junior role at a large client services firm, and while some senior folks were away on client assignments, she and a peer were tasked with preparing some material before a client pitch. The pair finished their assignment a few days early, but instead of sitting at the office playing solitaire, they pressed on, creating and organizing more materials and the pitch strategy. When the senior folks returned to the office the following week, my friend and her colleague shared their work. The senior team was so impressed that they used it during the actual pitch. It was all very exciting for the two junior folks.

In the end, however, the pitch wasn't successful. The client chose another firm, and my colleague and her peer were promoted. That's right. Rather than being incentivized by the result they could not control, they were being incentivized to continue doing what they could control—their behavior, initiative, and ownership. Leadership promoted them for those qualities. That's how you do it.

The more senior you are in an organization, the further you typically are from delivering the products or services on offer. Those on the front lines of your operation do the majority of that work. Thus, while every organization exists to serve an end user (the people and organizations that use the product or service), leaders are typically far removed from that end user and ought to prioritize serving their team members. That means listening to them, staying curious about their work, learning from them, removing obstacles for them, and creating greater opportunities.

When leaders show up to serve others, those people are more likely to serve each other, and that care almost always extends to customers and clients. And when customers and clients are happy, your bottom line is taken care of. That's what the order should be. That's capitalism at its finest.

Those who focus on the behaviors, processes, and policies that are in their control are more likely to understand that building a healthy organizational culture and achieving success are not mutually exclusive. In fact, they're very much linked. Take, for example, the case of DICK's Sporting Goods.

In the wake of the 2018 school shooting at Marjory Stoneman Douglas High School in Parkland, Florida, investigations revealed that the shooter had purchased a shotgun at DICK's. Though the shotgun wasn't used during the attack, the company's CEO, Ed Stack, announced that DICK's was making some big changes when it came to the products it carried. The stores would no longer sell assault-style weapons, high-capacity magazines, or "bump stocks," which could transform semi-automatic weapons into machine guns, and it would no longer sell guns to anyone under the age of twenty-one. "We've just decided that based on what's happened with these guns, we don't want to be part of the story and we've eliminated these guns permanently," he said.

The choice drew outrage from the National Rifle Association (NRA) and pro-gun politicians, but Stack was unfazed. "A number of people have said to me that this had to be a really hard decision. It was not," he said.

At first, DICK's felt the financial impact of the move. Same-store sales dropped by 3.1 percent that fiscal year. But Stack and the company kept its promise, and then doubled down.

In March 2019, DICK's announced it would be removing all remaining guns and ammunition from 125 of its 720 stores. And in March 2020, the company's leadership shared that it would pull all guns and ammunition from 440 more stores.

Ultimately, the company's decision to stick to its morals proved to be good for business. Rather than lose revenue as a result of its actions, after the March 2020 announcement, net sales rocketed to $2.6 billion, rising by 4.7 percent year over year, and the company's stock price rose 13 percent after it shared its plans. This is evidence that aligning what you say with what you do and making decisions based on what you can control to reflect your values pays off in numerous ways.

So, as you think about the leader you want to be—and the kind of organization you want to contribute to—examine the gaps between what you say and what you do. Do your decisions and behaviors align with your desired identity and values? If not, it's time to improve. And you don't have to do it alone.

If you're open to exploring gaps between what you say and what you do, you've come to the right place. Regardless of your level or experience, if you wish to lead in a way that guides you and your teammates with humility, ethics, and sustainable progress, you belong here. And if you want to feel great showing up to work, and to enable others to feel great too, because you all use your voices and bring your whole selves to the table—including ideas, passions, and even concerns, disagreements, and mistakes—this book is for you as well.

It Begins with Us

By now you've seen the ways in which a culture that shuts down its constituents isn't just demoralizing; it's dangerous. There can be dire consequences for the organization and—most importantly—for people. Boeing's and Ford's choices to prioritize profits resulted in many lives lost, along with reputational and financial damages, all of which were avoidable. On the flip side, a speak-up culture promotes an environment where individuals, innovation, and performance can thrive.

This book will show you how to change your environment from one in which you hear nothing but platitudes, complaints, or the sound of silence into a space where people feel it is both safe and worth it to share feedback, ideas, concerns, errors, and even dissent—where speaking up is encouraged and rewarded. Together, we'll explore why building a speak-up culture benefits both individuals and performance, the roadblocks that tend to get in the way, what has gone wrong and right in organizational culture and leadership at large, and how to overcome those issues and seize the opportunities ahead.

This personal and professional challenge begins with those at the helm of organizations. I hope to convey to you that building a speak-up culture is well worth the effort. So, let's move to an important incentive for this undertaking: speaking up is good for business.

2

Speaking Up Is Good for Business

*"When people don't want the best
for you, they are not the best for you."*
GAYLE KING

IT WAS February 11, 2021—nearly a year into COVID-19 pandemic life. I was in what had become a very familiar setting: my home office. I was stationed in front of my computer screen, lights and webcam on, with a snack just out of frame, dress shirt on top, sweatpants on the bottom, and slippers on my feet. So long as no one asked me to stand up, I was business casual.

That day, I was leading a virtual workshop for a sales organization at a large multinational corporation. I posed a series of questions I had been asking on repeat over the past several months as individuals and organizations of all sizes and industries navigated new territory. Until then, many of the participants' answers to these questions had been similar, but that day someone's response to one of the questions was particularly inspiring.

"What makes you feel proud to be part of this team?" I asked. Then I sent participants into virtual breakout rooms to discuss their answers.

As soon as everyone returned, one woman, Sofía, asked to share with the whole group what she had told those in her breakout room. From her tone and body language, I could already sense her eagerness and the emotion she was about to bring.

Before COVID, she told us, her leader, Luis—who oversaw sales in Central America and the Caribbean—would travel to meet with his leaders in their territories once a quarter. He'd fly in for the day, join them on their daily routine of sales calls and client site visits, and, over lunch, discuss how they and their business had been. While most of Luis's peers frequently skipped the quarterly trips altogether, Luis never missed one. He would purposefully take the first flight out, often well before the sun came up, to start the workday at eight in the morning, the same time his sales reps started out in the field. "Why should they flex to my schedule?" Luis would ask. He wanted to spend the full day with his people on their time, not his. Luis would use these in-person visits to help his leaders set goals—for themselves and the business—for the next quarter and beyond.

Now, during the pandemic, the paradigm had shifted. Luis's "trips" were over videoconference, with neither a customer nor bread to break in sight.

As Sofía's virtual meeting with Luis approached, she became increasingly nervous. As she was a single mother of two children attempting to do a field job from home, her capacity to excel in her role was significantly diminished—and it showed. Her numbers were way down. She feared this was it, that during the meeting Luis would tell her that he and the company would no longer need her services.

She decided she had to go on the offense, so she put together a PowerPoint presentation on what she'd do moving forward to improve her numbers and save her job.

It came time for the video call, and when Luis joined, she hastily greeted him and began sharing her screen.

"Sofía, what are you doing?" he asked.

"I wanted to share a PowerPoint," she said, "to explain my numbers."

"We're in a pandemic. You're a single mother of two children. We'd normally have lunch, drive around town together, and go on site visits," he said. "Turn it off. How are you? What do you need? What's happening?"

Sofía broke into tears.

Upon collecting herself, she replied, "This is the first time in my career I've ever been told that delivering the numbers isn't the most important thing." She then explained everything— the challenges of working from home in a role that was previously designed to be fulfilled on the road, the struggle of caring for her children and their virtual education full-time as she attempted to work, all wrapped in the uncertainty of the pandemic. She told Luis how it had affected her performance and how worried she'd been to have this call.

"Don't worry. Your job isn't at risk," he told her. "You're a good worker. You're a good person. You're a great teammate. We'll figure this out together. We'll make it work."

Both took a deep breath. The stress dissipated, and after the pause, Luis said, "Now you can show me that presentation."

Rather than coming in hot-headed and accusatory of her numbers at the top of the meeting, Luis created an environment where Sofía felt comfortable to speak up and share openly. By leading with care, Luis transformed the dynamic. And that meant they could address her struggles together—a joint effort that improved her experience, her life, *and* the company's bottom line.

Sofía became one of the highest performers and greatest cultural champions in this new hybrid world of work in the quarters that followed. As of this writing, she is preparing to go on maternity leave for her third child and has continued her cultural leadership as an advocate for work-life integration for working parents, especially mothers.

Thanks to Luis's compassion and willingness to lead, Sofía became determined to do better—not because she feared losing her job, but because she cared even more deeply about her role, the organization, and its leadership. It's just one example of how a leader can help someone flip their feelings of fear to ones of trust, loyalty, and wanting to give of their discretionary effort.

The Power and Benefits of a Speak-Up Culture

By inspiring and supporting those in their span of care, leaders can affect long-term and sustainable results. And the data reflects this truth. Researchers at the Center for Talent Innovation found that "a diverse workforce that's managed by leaders who cherish difference, embrace disruption, and foster a speak-up culture ... [enable] companies to increase their share of existing markets and lever open brand-new ones. By encouraging a proliferation of perspectives, leaders who foster a speak-up culture also enable companies to realize greater efficiencies and trim costs" directly impacting the bottom line. They found that companies with speak-up cultures were 70 percent more likely to capture new markets and 45 percent more likely to have grown their market share than those without them. And, for anyone who thinks speaking up works only in certain cultures, this research came from studying eleven growth markets, including those in Brazil, China, Hong Kong, India, Japan, Russia, Singapore, South Africa, Turkey, the United Kingdom, and the United States.

For a quintessential example of the power and benefits of a speak-up culture, we can look to the case of former Boeing executive Alan Mulally and his tenure at Ford Motor Company.

Mulally began his career with Boeing as an engineer in 1969, eventually becoming the CEO of Boeing Commercial Airplanes. He was largely credited with Boeing Commercial's resurgence in the mid-2000s before he took the helm at the then mightily struggling Ford Motor Company. In the fifteen years before Mulally took over, Ford had lost 25 percent of its market share and was headed toward bankruptcy.

At the formal press conference to announce his new role, a reporter asked him what kind of car he drove. "A Lexus," Mulally responded, "It's the finest car in the world." This was a rallying cry to challenge Ford employees to make a car Mulally wanted to drive.

As expected of a leader in a new role, Mulally set up a series of weekly status report meetings with senior executives at the company. He wanted to get a sense of what was working and what wasn't. Initially, he was surprised that all the reports from executives were positive. After weeks of this charade, a frustrated Mulally said, "We are going to lose billions of dollars this year." He told them that the company was bleeding money; there was no way everything was hunky-dory. He shared that he, the whole room of leaders, and the organization needed to embrace more truth telling if they were to legitimately improve and save the company.

There was a good reason the executives gave the reports they did. The previous CEO had a very different style of leadership from Mulally, and the executives were conditioned to behave a certain way. Mulally had work to do to create the type of environment that encouraged and rewarded people for speaking up with their ideas, concerns, disagreements, and mistakes. But he kept at it, believing it was the way forward.

Eventually, one person, Mark Fields, head of operations in the Americas at the time, gave a status update that was anything other than rosy—the first in Mulally's tenure. Mulally apparently stood up, gave Fields a standing ovation, and asked the

When people feel cared for, they are more likely to extend that care to others.

room who could help Fields solve his issue. Someone else raised their hand and a new precedent was set.

To further reward the behavior, Mulally insisted that Fields sit directly next to him at the next meeting. In July 2014, Fields ended up succeeding Mulally as the next president and CEO. Through Alan Mulally's leadership, Ford returned to profitability and became the only major American car manufacturer to avoid a government bailout following the 2008 stock market crash.

I'm often asked to identify organizations that have great speak-up cultures, and I'm hesitant to answer. It's harder to evaluate organizations and easier to evaluate leaders. Take Microsoft as an example. Under Bill Gates, Microsoft was very different from how it was under the highly competitive Steve Ballmer, and it's different again under the leadership of Satya Nadella. I've heard Nadella speak and I like what I hear. He talks about helping Microsoft "rediscover its soul"; he prioritizes empathy and humility, striving to create a *learn-it-all* rather than *know-it-all* culture. Nadella also expects that leaders at Microsoft *model* the culture and values in their actions; *coach* their team members to define objectives, adapt, and learn; and *care* deeply for their employees, seeking to understand their capabilities and ambitions and to invest in their growth. This isn't to say that Nadella, Microsoft, or any leader or organization is perfect. That's impossible. Nor does it mean that every single leader at Microsoft is a match for everyone. But if more leaders, especially the most senior leaders, consistently *model*, *coach*, and *care*, they are more likely to proliferate a healthy speak-up culture.

Affection for Those in Your Charge

That leaders should care about those in their charge is not a new concept. *The Master of Demon Valley*, an ancient Chinese text on the philosophy of power dating back to the first millennium BCE, observes, "One with talent but no kindness cannot command an army."

This sentiment is brought to life with the US Marine Corps. Their 14 Leadership Traits—which were originally detailed in a 1948 army pamphlet—include justice, loyalty, tact, and unselfishness, all of which describe the ways in which marines interact with others. And eight of the 11 Marine Corps Leadership Principles (first laid out in 1951) describe an obligation to one's peers and subordinates:

- Know your Marines and look out for their welfare.

- Keep your Marines informed.

- Set the example.

- Ensure the task is understood, supervised, and accomplished.

- Train your Marines as a team.

- Develop a sense of responsibility among your subordinates.

- Employ your command in accordance with its capabilities.

- Seek responsibility and take responsibility for your actions.

At the core of these philosophies is an unwritten code about what it means to be a leader of US Marines—you must find affection for those in your care. This means leaders must be able to find, appreciate, and cultivate the strengths, genius, and worth in the members of their team. If you aren't willing or able to see that in someone who is in your span of care, I have news for you: you aren't fit to lead that person.

Data from Gallup backs this up. A study led by Susan Sorenson found that when managers ignored their employees, 40 percent of those employees were actively disengaged. Managers who pointed out only their employees' weaknesses cut active disengagement to 22 percent. The figure improved by nearly half when managers simply acknowledged that their team members existed. Fear not—there is hope. Supervisors who pointed out and cultivated their direct reports' strengths dramatically increased engagement, such that only 1 percent of employees were disengaged. No office bean bag chairs, Ping-Pong tables, free lunch, or corporate swag sent to someone's home. Herein lies a *hack* to employee engagement—good old sound leadership.

You won't feel affection toward everyone you lead. By the same token, not everyone is a good addition to your team or match with your leadership style. That's fine—some individuals may belong better with another leader, be it in another team, department, or organization altogether. But if you're after real success, you must approach your people not as cogs in a machine but as human beings who are critical to your operations.

Yup. This means more work because leadership is not an easy job and not for the faint of heart. It means you ought to listen, seek others' input, and take it in. You ought to ask more questions and answer more of them as well. And when you do answer, share honestly and with as much transparency as you can. Vulnerability doesn't mean sharing everything—that could simply be oversharing. Vulnerability does mean sharing what is relevant, which includes admitting when you don't yet know an answer or need help. Your team will feel the effects of your efforts, consistency, and sincerity. They'll know you care, and that can make a world of difference to them as individuals and to your teams and organization. Further, these types of behaviors displayed by leaders are positively contagious.

When people feel you care, they're more likely to extend that care to others and bring their whole selves to work, including their ideas, concerns, disagreements, and mistakes. The result? Engagement, buy-in, discretionary effort, healthier cultures, and continuous improvement—all of which have the potential to make your organization better, safer, stronger, and more fun, human, and adaptable.

In organizations with speak-up cultures, people feel it is both safe and worth it to share their opinions openly while still being respectful. Trust and collaboration thrive and become the norm and, thus, information of all forms is seen as something that can improve the work, results, and our relationships. We share information not to blame and throw others under the bus, but to support one another and constantly advance our relationships and work.

I should note, too, that the alternative is bleak. Absent a speak-up culture, people tend to hide bad news for fear of how it may be received and potentially harm them. Or they may view useful information as a source of power and security. To protect themselves, they may hoard it for personal and strategic use instead of sharing it to benefit others and the organization as a whole. This creates a culture of fear and scarcity rather than one of sharing, sincerity, generosity, selflessness, and trust.

When people feel cared for, they are more likely to extend that care to others, including colleagues, clients, and vendors. When they don't feel cared for, they're less likely to care for others and often become careless themselves.

I Didn't Put the Sponge in Their Liver!

Harvard Business School professor Amy Edmondson addressed the concept of psychological safety with a study of hospital units, where the impact of speaking up, yet again, can be life or death. She surveyed healthcare workers at eight units, looking at how psychologically safe their environments were and how many medication errors they made. She defines psychological safety as "a shared belief held by members of a team that the team is safe for interpersonal risk taking," and found that the more psychologically safe an environment seemed to be, the more medication errors were reported. Come again?!

On the surface, that seems like a dangerous connection. Perhaps a psychologically safe environment was conducive to slacking off and carelessness? Edmondson didn't think that was the case. Instead, she believed that at the hospitals with more psychological safety, people were more comfortable *reporting* their errors.

When she dug deeper, reviewing independent data about how many errors were made, not just reported, on the hospital units she surveyed, she found that those with high psychological safety indeed had *fewer* errors than their less psychologically safe counterparts. When psychological safety was lower, people went out of their way to hide mistakes from each other and their superiors for fear of reprimand. That meant worse outcomes for their patients because the workers spent more time sweeping their errors under the rug than improving the standard of care they offered.

While mistakes can be dangerous, particularly in a health-care setting, identifying and learning from them is key to innovation. The late psychologist Richard Farson and author Ralph Keyes touted the benefits of what they called failure-tolerant leaders, "executives who, through their words and actions, help people overcome their fear of failure and, in the process, create a culture of intelligent risk taking that leads to sustained innovation." In the case of the hospitals in Edmondson's study, that might mean new systems and processes to prevent medical errors.

An example of one such innovation is highlighted in Nir Eyal's 2019 book *Indistractable*, in which he describes a team of nurses who avoided medication errors by wearing signs instructing others not to interrupt them while they were doling out medications. As a result, they saw errors go down. Progress like this could come only from a culture in which team members willingly share their ideas, concerns, mistakes, and opportunities to improve. And in even the most supportive and healthy environment, that can be scary—which brings us to another truth.

Low Fear, Not No Fear

Having a speak-up culture is not about feeling warm and fuzzy all the time. While that may sound utopian, it's more "faux-topian"—a fantasy in which no one is ever uncomfortable, upset, or afraid. Psychological safety, a fundamental characteristic of a speak-up culture, is depicted by high candor and *low* fear, not *no* fear. Fearlessness doesn't really exist. And if it does, it's dangerous. Fear is designed to keep us alert and safe. The leaders among us feel the fear and press on anyway because they are connected to something bigger than themselves and more important than the fear itself. In fact, if it weren't for fear, we wouldn't need courage. We need to create cultures in which people show up even when they are afraid because they know they will be encouraged and rewarded for sharing their ideas, concerns, disagreements, and mistakes, and for acting with courage and integrity. Again, the goal is not to be fearless. There is no such thing as the "fearless leader." The goal is for leaders to create less fear.

The late IBM chairman and CEO Thomas Watson once said, "The fastest way to succeed is to double your failure rate." To do that, we must not only encourage innovation, but also create a space in which people can admit their missteps. To innovate we must experiment. A natural and fundamental result of experimentation is failure. If we punish people for failing, guess what? We don't get innovation.

So, if speaking up is such a good thing, why isn't it ubiquitous? And what if you're expecting people to speak up and they don't? Leaders at organizations of all sizes have asked me some version of those questions, and the answer is simple. As the person at the top, you set the tone—and that means if you truly want a speak-up culture, it behooves you to go first.

Farson and Keyes wrote that L.D. DeSimone, former CEO of 3M, frequently shared one of his failures. "He never hesitated to recount how he repeatedly tried to stop the development of Thinsulate [a trademarked brand of thermal insulation made of synthetic fiber and used in clothing]. Luckily, DeSimone failed and Thinsulate became one of the company's most successful products. By being so candid about his near blunder," Farson and Keyes explained, "DeSimone powerfully conveyed that it's okay to be wrong and admit when you are." In fact, as we'll explore in the next chapter, it's not only okay; it's essential.

3

Speak Up,
Why Don't You?

*"The biggest concern for any
organization should be when their most
passionate people become quiet."*

TIM MCCLURE

THINK BACK to a time when a leader told you, "My door is always open."

Did you believe them? More importantly, did you do anything about it?

Now, consider if you've ever said the same thing—and whether your team members took you up on the offer to drop in or schedule a time to have a candid conversation.

If they did stop by, what happened? Did you give them the time of day? Did the conversation stay at the surface or was there depth? Did you encourage and reward them for showing up and sharing their truth?

Those who say "my door is always open" assume that their team members feel confident, capable, and psychologically safe enough to come to the door, and that it's worth their breath when they do. If leaders have created an environment that doesn't support those conditions, no one's likely to come to the door, whether it's open or not.

Management and organization researchers Hemant Kakkar and Subra Tangirala's findings confirm this. They dug into the two leading viewpoints on why people don't speak up. One is that personality dictates the behavior; this perspective assumes that staying silent about critical issues is part of one's disposition. The other predominant view is that the work environment itself prevents people from raising concerns. Kakkar and Tangirala surveyed 291 employees and supervisors across thirty-five teams at a manufacturing plant. They assessed employees' personalities, whether speaking up was expected as part of their work, and whether it was rewarded or punished. Then they asked supervisors how frequently each person spoke up.

While they learned that both personality and situation influenced one's tendency to share, they

> found that strong environmental norms could override the influence of personality on employees' willingness to speak up at work ... This finding suggests that if you want employees to speak up, the work environment and the team's social norms matter. Even people who are most inclined to raise ideas and suggestions may not do so if they fear being put down or penalized. On the flip side, encouraging and rewarding speaking up can help more people do so, even if their personality makes them more risk-averse.

A person's day-to-day environment affects how they behave. Put a highly trustworthy individual in an unhealthy culture and it will undoubtedly impact them—their behavior, their well-being, and their performance. The opposite also holds true.

Thought of in a different (and fermented) way, if you put a cucumber in pickle brine, ten times out of ten that thing turns into a pickle. And I think we can all agree that some pickles—

to whatever your taste (crunchy, sweet, dill, bread and butter, kosher, sour, and beyond)—are nature's miracle, while some never should have been jarred. Our environment, culture, and surroundings influence our behavior, both positively and negatively. I jokingly, or not so jokingly, refer to this as pickle theory (hashtag as you wish). What's the pickle brine in your organization? Do your teams, leadership, systems, and culture make people better or worse off?

We can take a page from my client Rita Sanna's playbook. Sanna is an operations director at a multinational engineering firm. She is based in Dubai and works directly with a team based in India on several projects. India has a historically deferential culture, and Sanna observed that the India-based team had inadvertently taken a subordinate position to the Dubai team— they were holding back from speaking up. Sanna knew this dynamic would be ineffective for the results she needed to lead. Both teams would need to show up fully and as equals to achieve the desired outcomes. So, she insisted that the next in-person team gathering take place in India and not Dubai, which she discerned would send a message of equality. At this next meeting in India, she introduced what she called a "speak-up moment" that would occur during every team meeting (in-person and virtual) starting then and moving forward. The goal was to share smoke before it became fire.

Sanna and the teams developed and agreed upon rules about how every participant would engage. To begin with, these agreements were:

- Stay curious—this is not a time to shrink or defend, this is a time to become and stay curious.

- Treat everyone with respect—no one is allowed to roll their eyes or show up in a dismissive or submissive way to one another.

- Dissect and critique ideas, not people.

- Ensure speak-up moments are included in every meeting.

With Sanna's leadership, the teams created a new norm that transcended the cultural challenges.

Those speak-up moments provided the teams with the space to show up and share something that needed to be said—ideas, concerns, disagreements, and mistakes. And the regular sessions and designed moments formed a systematized ritual and cultural norm of speaking up.

A bonus? It cost exactly zero additional dollars to execute on this, while creating a tremendous impact. Speaking up has become a cultural habit that continues to pay dividends.

Where Did All the Office Doors Go?

The need to cultivate a speak-up culture becomes ever more pressing as many organizations embrace remote and hybrid work environments. Videoconferencing has made physical office doors fewer and farther between and sometimes non-existent. This shift in the way we work has demonstrated how inaccessible many of those open-door invitations were, and how much harder we now must work to encourage people to speak up and ensure they feel it's both safe enough and worth it to do so.

"My door is always open" is passive leadership. Active leadership is roaming the halls—literally and virtually—to see what support people need, knowing one size does not fit all. Instead of waiting for people to come to them, leaders ought to be active in their role of supporting people.

As early as kindergarten, we're taught the Golden Rule. And while many of us live by it—treating others as *we* want to be treated—this approach lacks empathy. If we want to cultivate a speak-up culture, we must embody the Platinum Rule: treat people as *they* wish to be treated. To do that, we must observe, ask them what they need, and truly listen and act—particularly in a remote workplace.

So much of relationship-building and culture occurs during the pauses in our day—the moments of serendipity that occur much more readily and easily in person. Picture this: You and I are attending the same in-person meeting. During a scheduled coffee break, we both reach for the same cranberry muffin on a pastry platter.

"Cranberry muffin?" you ask.

"Yeah, I love them!" I reply.

"Me too!" you say, and we instantly become cranberry muffin companions from then on. What happens in that moment is so much bigger than a shared affinity for simple carbohydrates and tart antioxidants. It's a point of connection, an element of our shared humanity that lays the foundation for us to broach much more difficult subjects when the need arises. Some months or years down the road, a tension- and pressure-filled exchange could be defused and put into perspective with a simple comment like, "Gosh, I could really go for a cranberry muffin right about now." That humor, recollection, and connection is worth its weight in platinum.

Though we have plenty of platforms for *interaction* in a remote environment—videoconferencing, audio, project management, scheduling, social media, and other communication and "productivity" tools—moments of serendipity are harder to come by, if they happen at all.

Many remote companies hold videoconferences that are much larger than their in-person predecessors because the technological tools at our fingertips enable us to thwart the rules of time and space. Senior leaders may gather teams from around the country, and even the world, to share updates, bringing together strangers across departments and time zones. Sometimes we can see the faces of our cross-country or global counterparts. Other times, with large meetings gathering tens, hundreds, or even thousands, there isn't much difference between our organizational update meetings and watching the six o'clock news broadcast.

The size of the group also affects people's willingness to speak up, and the likelihood that they'll be heard. Researchers Gus Cooney, Adam Mastroianni, Nicole Abi-Esber, and Alison Wood Brooks found that group size significantly affects what and how much people are willing to disclose and how they feel about what they share. This is called a many minds problem: each added mind "fundamentally alters the basics of conversation."

As a result, leaders often find themselves smack-dab in the middle of a bobblehead culture—met with a sea of (sometimes) smiling, nodding heads who all happen to be on mute. Leaders are at risk of confusing those muted microphones and nodding heads for consensus. But it isn't consensus. It's far more likely to be "nice," convenient, or polite silence, and it can be dangerous. At its most innocuous, you miss out on ideas, feedback, and opportunities that could have otherwise been shared. At its most harmful, it can cause failure or even devastation, as previous examples attest.

An even greater challenge than muted microphones is when some, most, or all participants turn off their videos altogether. Leaders ask for questions, count down from three, and move right along, assuming everyone is on the same page. Or they press on to avoid the awkward silence, perhaps feeling depleted by the challenge of engaging their virtual teams.

This is not to say that the *only* way to foster a speak-up culture is through in-person meetings and buttering people up with muffins and pastries. There are numerous ways to employ technology to ensure everyone can provide honest, real, and useful feedback. I have seen leaders and teams use:

- The chat function, polls, and other tools for interaction, to gain real-time feedback and incorporate people's questions, ideas, concerns, and challenges.

- Requests for people to turn their videos on to increase interaction, communication, and connection, building in ample breaks from screen time.

- Walking phone calls for one-on-one meetings, if appropriate and possible.

- Breakout rooms to garner discussion. Some teams put senior leaders or facilitators in each room to elicit dialogue, hear from everyone, answer questions, embrace silence, and gain useful feedback. The purpose of every breakout discussion should be some sort of report out. If you break out and don't debrief, why did you break out in the first place? If you don't have the time, space, or setup for participants to share by voice, use the chat function to answer prompts for discussion and capture outstanding questions. Input gained from the breakout sessions and debrief discussions can and should inform the work ahead.

- Quantitative tools via polls, chat, or otherwise, such as asking, "On a scale of zero to ten, how clear was that presentation? And if you all say ten, I'll think you're lying [said in jest]. I want real feedback, I want to improve, and I want to be effective for you." And when people answer honestly and provide reasoning for their rating, leaders ought to celebrate and reward that truth being shared. This is not the time to be defensive. This is the time to appreciate realness and honesty.

- Analog cards for an express check-in. To begin meetings or at intervals, teams can flash different colored cards to express how they're feeling. For example, red is overwhelmed, yellow is just full, and green communicates capacity. Team leaders and members can then quickly figure out who needs support and where people are at. They can also track this over time to see who may be struggling, who has too much on their plate, and who needs training or other ongoing support.

Those are just a handful of ideas to foster a speak-up culture, specifically in a virtual setting. And as you know, environment matters. So, whether at a virtual, in-person, or hybrid meeting, if you truly value the input from your attendees, share that hope and expectation with them at the outset of the meeting. Share with them that their feedback and contributions are necessary, expected, and essential (only if they truly are . . . and they'll find out either way). Encourage them to speak up—use open-ended questions and silence, making room for them—and when people do share, reward them for it, if indeed you wish to hear their voices, and other voices, again.

To Speak Up or Not to Speak Up?

When we join a team, we very quickly learn the culture and norms—what's accepted and what's not. We may hear about someone else's attempt to share an idea, concern, disagreement, or mistake. Perhaps it went well; perhaps it didn't. We may even be so bold as to contribute to a conversation. What happens next typically dictates how we, and others, will behave going forward.

Some may speak up and be encouraged and rewarded for doing so (we'll dig into the value of encouraging and rewarding others in chapter 8). Still, people may speak up and be ignored or, worse, punished. Some may never find out how leadership would react to what they are thinking because they do the

If we want to cultivate a speak-up culture, we must embody **the Platinum Rule: treat people as *they* wish to be treated.**

math in their head and choose to refrain from speaking up at all. When people choose not to speak up, they tend to hold back for two reasons: fear and/or apathy.

Is It Safe? Is It Worth It?

Before someone chooses to speak up, they consciously or unconsciously ask themselves:

- **Is it safe?** Do I feel there is enough psychological safety present for me to take the risk to my job, relationships, and reputation to speak up?

- **Is it worth it?** Do I perceive that speaking up will yield a useful, positive impact? (This is what's known as "perceived impact.")

The graph above maps out the continua of fear to safety and apathy to impact. Obviously, the top-right quadrant is the sweet spot. When safety and impact are high and maintained, you're likely have a healthy speak-up culture. Again, this is not a place of fearlessness, but rather a place where people fear less. The bottom left is a miserable place to be. I've been there and I've seen others there as well. It's an unhappy marriage between fear and apathy, where it feels neither safe nor worth it to speak up. Quiet quitting (putting one's head down, doing the bare minimum, waiting until something better comes along) or resignation likely happens here. The other two quadrants are less straightforward. The top left is characterized by safety, but low impact. You may feel safe to confront a friend, colleague, or boss, but you do not believe doing so would lead to any meaningful change. Perhaps this is because of bureaucracy, a larger systemic issue, or because a personal change in habits would be highly improbable.

The final quadrant in the bottom right—low safety and high impact—is where Ed Pierson, the senior manager at Boeing, found himself. The cost of remaining silent was too high. This is the reason a speak-up culture is ever more important in high-stakes and potentially dangerous lines of work and environments. Pierson and others courageously risked their jobs, livelihoods, reputations, and relationships to speak up. In his case, after repeated attempts and dead ends, Pierson ultimately decided to whistleblow, testifying before the US Congress.

This was also the case for Kimberly Young-McLear, a whistleblower who served in the US Coast Guard from 2003 to 2023. As a queer Black woman with a PhD and highly decorated in the Coast Guard, she was unfortunately the target of workplace bullying, psychological harassment, and intimidation. Young-McLear felt harassed because she brought a differing opinion and point of view, because of her gender, race, sexual orientation, and same-sex marriage, and because she became a trusted confidante across the Coast Guard. In 2016, after enduring two years of direct abuse, she made the conscious decision to speak up, "not only for [her] own survival," but also to shine a light and educate others on the injustices she felt and saw were occurring more broadly in the organization. Following her speaking up as a whistleblower, she experienced further retaliation. Today, Young-McLear continues to be an outspoken advocate for helping leaders and organizations create workplaces and communities where people feel they matter, belong, and can be their full, authentic, and healthiest selves.

Is It Safe?

When people are afraid that something bad will happen to them because of their decision to speak up, in most cases, they won't do it. And can we really blame them? This is, seemingly, leadership's failure to foster the type of culture that encourages and rewards people for speaking up.

Whether our experience is real or perceived—and sometimes our perception is our reality—if it feels dangerous and that we may be punished for sharing our ideas, concerns, disagreements, and mistakes, the likelihood of our speaking up decreases. Professors Ethan Burris and Jim Detert call the process of deciding whether to speak up "voice calculus," during which people "weigh the expected success and benefits of speaking up against the risks."

Two psychological phenomena that affect the outcome of our voice calculus and a propensity for staying quiet are gaslighting and toxic positivity.

Gaslighting occurs when someone is manipulated by psychological means into questioning their own reality. Sounds fun, I know. For example: someone dares to risk sharing with their leader how they feel and their leader essentially responds with, "You're incorrect. You don't feel that way." Of course, this is a ridiculous assertion. While we can debate facts and figures, arguing that someone's feelings are invalid is quite inhumane and certainly lacks emotional intelligence.

A "gaslighter" uses four main techniques (with examples) to influence their victim:

1 Reality manipulation ("that's not what happened")

2 Scapegoating ("you are the problem" or "they are the problem")

3 A straight-up lie ("this contract is designed to protect you")

4 Coercion ("do this, or else")

Convincing others that they themselves are the problem rather than acknowledging and dealing appropriately with the very issue they are raising is a form of gaslighting. This is also abdicating the responsibility of leadership.

Toxic positivity is a more subtle cousin, if you will, of gaslighting. It's a "good vibes only" approach, where we're allowed to talk only about good things and the future—no lamenting about the past or talking about the real challenges at hand. For example: 30 percent of the workforce was just laid off and talking about it to cope and grieve is off-limits: "Are you a part of the problem or do you want to be a part of the solution?" people may say.

Blind positivity is not the same thing as grounded and realistic optimism. Toxic positivity is the belief that people should always remain positive, no matter how dire the circumstances. Wishing negativity away is not a great strategy. The avoidance of those hard and real emotions is unproductive and unhealthy. Toxic positivity is dysfunctional emotional management, without the full acknowledgment of negative emotions, particularly anger and sadness. These, of course, are part of the full spectrum of human emotions.

When organizations encourage and reward people for sharing how they truly feel and make space for expressing emotions beyond the positive ones, it can be an advantage. As Susan David teaches us in her 2016 book, *Emotional Agility*, emotions are data that can inform us and others of what's going on. When a broader spectrum of emotions is safe and welcome within organizations, we can make better, more sound, holistic, and wise decisions.

To avoid gaslighting or toxic positivity—and, perhaps most pressingly, being fired—people turn the other cheek, put their head down, share the truth but not the whole truth, or just keep walking by. Importantly, it doesn't matter whether their fears are well-founded or not.

Again, our truth is but our perception. Our brain releases cortisol whenever we sense a threat. Cortisol is the same neurochemical that during our primal days instigated us to either head for the hills or stay and fight. While our surroundings have evolved, our neurobiology hasn't. When we perceive a threat, our brains release cortisol—our pupils dilate and our muscles tense just as readily inside the four walls of our office or videoconference screen as they did on the plains. The only difference is that now we're worried about losing our livelihood, not about being eaten by a large cat. But it feels as critical, as if we were worried for our lives. Cortisol is, after all, designed to keep us safe. If it feels dangerous to speak up, the likelihood that we will diminishes.

Is It Worth It?

Sometimes people don't speak up out of apathy. They lack enthusiasm, interest, or concern for their workplace. They feel as if speaking up won't make a difference, or that sharing their opinion may make things worse. Or people may use their voice, but the quality and truth of what they're sharing is diminished if they don't feel their truth will be rewarded or well received.

Much like fear, apathy can be a form of self-protection and preservation. Someone may become apathetic if they or a peer tried to speak up and it either blew up in their face or created no change at all, even after repeated attempts. Apathy spreads when people perceive that their organization does not do well with bad news or challenges to the status quo. This could be due to leadership behaviors and/or structural and systemic issues like bureaucracy or discrimination. And if you have a culture where only certain people's voices and not others are heard, both apathy and fear can set in.

When apathy and fear are present, people often look for a way out. A friend of mine saw the writing on the wall at her job. A new leadership team came in, and as the culture began to shift toward something that felt quite sinister, she was sure that she would eventually be fired. She quietly quit, deciding she'd put in minimal effort while she looked for something new. It became a race with her employer to see who wouldn't need the other first.

And she's not alone. While a record number of people quit their jobs in search of better working environments during the COVID-19 pandemic—47.8 million US employees in 2021 alone—many others have been biding their time, present but checked out, with nine toes out the door as they wait for a better opportunity. And by "better" I mean with greater flexibility, fair compensation, and healthy leaders and organizational cultures.

According to Gallup, as of April 2022, just 36 percent of US workers were engaged in their jobs. Meanwhile, 74 percent of disengaged workers were looking for new roles, compared to 30 percent of engaged employees looking for new opportunities. Although employees looking for new roles is not equal to a reduction in head count, employers are losing out on the benefits of an engaged workforce, such as discretionary effort, new ideas, loyalty, and more, including an estimated $450 to $500 billion in lost productivity per year in the United States alone. Globally, employees who are not engaged or who are actively disengaged create a global cost of $7.8 trillion in lost productivity, according to Gallup's *State of the Global Workplace: 2022 Report.* That's equal to 11 percent of the world's GDP.

What's My Damage?

Although the environment is primarily responsible for whether people speak up, we must also consider what individuals bring with them to any situation. After all, we don't start a new role in a vacuum. Our past experiences shape the way we respond, even when we move to a different leader, organization, or work culture. Psychologist, business strategist, and author Liane Davey explains that individuals must ask, "Am I safe from myself?" We all ought to consider whether we or others are acting (or failing to act) because of residual discomfort from previous relationships.

Maybe a member of your team's parents primed them to believe they shouldn't make a fuss regardless of their circumstances, or their friends painted them as the stoic or the supportive sidekick. Perhaps they have a wonderful boss today (go, you!), but they don't speak up because their past three supervisors were ill-equipped leaders who shut them down whenever they attempted to raise an idea, concern, disagreement, or mistake.

I certainly don't blame them for holding back; we're all products of our conditioning. But their hesitancy to speak up, whether out of fear or apathy, has less to do with the objective environment they are in and more to do with their own perception of safety and impact.

Further, if they are fearful that when they share an idea people will ask them tough questions or request that they back it up with research, or they sit in the back of the room because they don't want to be put on the spot, that may reflect less about the environment and more about them. Davey calls this "fear of aversive outcomes."

We can all do the work of assessing the origins of our discomfort or disinterest and proceed accordingly. This need not be a solo pursuit. Gaining from the objective perspectives of friends, colleagues, coaches, therapists, and the like can most definitely help.

That people often step into your culture with their own prior baggage makes it even more necessary for you to create an environment in which they feel safe, consistently and over time. But cultivating a speak-up culture doesn't mean we're nice to each other all the time. It's not a culture of hearts, XOXOs, sunshine and rainbows, free lollipops in the cafeteria, and kumbaya sessions in the boardroom. Quite the opposite: in a speak-up culture, we can have the hardest conversations there are. As we'll discuss in chapter 9, that is candor with care.

So many of the issues and opportunities we have already explored highlight the role and importance of culture. Leaders set that tone. Establishing a speak-up culture requires that individuals, teams, and organizations understand what leadership *really* means—and who is equipped to do it.

4

Leadership Defined

"Leadership is hard to define and good leadership even harder. But if you can get people to follow you to the ends of the earth, you are a great leader."
INDRA NOOYI

"**D**AD, I got the job!"

It was November 2008. I was in my final year of a business management program, and I'd just gotten the call I'd been waiting for: I had secured a full-time job following my graduation, with a major corporation in their leadership development program. I was elated. My first call after that was to my parents. My father picked up the phone, and as I shared the great news with him, I could tell that he, a man who tends to be reserved with his emotions, was thrilled too. It sounded as if he was on the verge of tears on the other end of the line. His pride was palpable, and that meant the world to me.

I made my way through the rest of the semester and into the next. There wasn't much to worry about; after all, I'd lined up my plans for life after graduation.

But one Sunday night in March 2009, one of my roommates delivered some concerning news.

"Heads up," he said from behind his computer screen in the other room. "Your company just went through a merger."

A merger?! A quick Internet search confirmed what he'd said, and there was much speculation about what that would mean for my future employer and the fate of its employees—me included.

The next day, I was back in class. I glanced at my phone during a scheduled break and saw that I had missed a call and had a voicemail from a number I didn't recognize, but with a familiar area code. I stepped out into a quiet stairway to listen to the voice message. It was from my human resources rep, Abi, at my employer-to-be, asking me to return her call ASAP.

My heart sank. I was sure I was fired, and before I had even started! I held my breath, my heart beating in my ears, as the phone rang. Abi picked up and I eked out my name and said that I was returning her call.

"Oh, hi," she responded. "I just want to let you know that your offer of employment still stands." I asked Abi to repeat herself and confirm the meaning of her sentence to ensure I heard her properly. Upon confirmation, I breathed a sigh of relief, thanked her profusely, and closed out the school year confident that my job was safe enough.

I awoke on September 7, 2009, bright-eyed and bushy-tailed, thrilled to start my full-time career. But as I ate my breakfast that morning, I saw a new set of headlines about my employer: one thousand people had been let go. The organization cited post-merger "efficiencies" by way of explanation. That day, I was the young whippersnapper walking in for the first time as many more people were walking out for the last time, boxes in hand.

It was quite a scene, and it continued to unfold in the weeks and months that followed. I saw firsthand the influence that leaders, culture, and a lack of transparency had on people, their feelings of psychological safety, and their perceived impact. This was despite positive intention from leaders—though we know that there can be a difference between intent and impact.

I distinctively remember Bryn, a thirty-seven-year veteran of the company, sitting fearfully in her cubicle, worrying that her pink slip would arrive next. Not only was her work productivity affected but also her mental and physical well-being. And that same anxiety extended to the rest of the team.

We were not experiencing great leadership; it felt far more like "leadershit," meaning too many people in positions of power were seemingly putting their own needs, safety, security, future, and well-being ahead of those in their span of care. I experienced many leaders in self-preservation mode rather than being there to serve, care, communicate, and own their impact. This is counter to what the responsibility of leadership ought to be. The leaders were, unfortunately, contributing toward an erosion of trust with the employee population.

There was at least one exception I clearly recall—a senior manager who was months from retirement. Like a second-term president who had nothing to lose, save for their legacy, this manager displayed the courage to put it all on the line for his people. He fought for the well-being of his team and each team member's future. He advocated for them to keep their jobs and have roles that suited their strengths. He communicated clearly, diplomatically, appropriately, and respectfully. He shared as much as he could. I cared for this leader because I knew he cared for us.

Countless organizations are struggling to overcome the impact of poor leadership.

Search for shining examples of leadership in our current organizational and societal landscape, and you're likely to come up with just a few. Most of us have perhaps only one or two leaders we would consider great in our careers, in their entirety! What a low bar. Even those running the world's most successful companies are often faced with valid criticism about toxic cultures, poor labor and business practices, and inadequate compensation.

I have some empathy for the overarching pickle brine that business executives, particularly in public companies, are in—a broken system of capitalism that is in dire need of restoration. In 1976, the late American economist and statistician Milton Friedman received the Nobel Memorial Prize in Economic Sciences. He developed a profit-centered definition of the social responsibility of business: "greed is good." The responsibility of business, he maintained, is to maximize profit and shareholder value while staying within the bounds of the law and ethical custom. Thanks to Friedman's theories—which were also made popular in large part due to the practices of Jack Welch at General Electric—laying off tens, hundreds, or even thousands of people based on the organization's financial performance alone has become customary. Today, we see that after an organization irresponsibly hires too aggressively or doesn't meet its fiscal goals or analyst targets, even if the business is profitable, it may still conduct mass layoffs. While that may be legal and has become customary, it's not necessarily ethical. We need a better standard and better definition of the social responsibility of business and leadership—one that prioritizes people, purpose, and then profit, in that order.

Make no mistake, I believe in capitalism. I simply believe in a better version of it. When we put people first, we must live our purpose from the inside out of our organizations. And profit prioritized third rather than first or second means that it exists as lifeblood to support people and advance the business' purpose.

But just because we lack an abundance of role models of ethical leadership and operate within a system that can prioritize profits doesn't mean leaders want to do a bad job. Most leaders are in it for the right reasons. They want to do right by their organizations, those they serve, *and* the people they employ. Yet, even those with the best of intentions find themselves struggling—and sometimes failing.

So, why do leaders let their people, and even society, down when they don't want to?

Leadership is not an easy job. And though it's never been smooth sailing, being a leader at this moment in history is particularly complex. We are finally recognizing the importance of humane, people-first, and purpose-driven leadership. We are learning to reconcile that with work cultures that prize the easy-to-measure productivity above all else, including our humanity. One of the primary issues leaders run into when they attempt to do better is quite simple: they struggle to find a standard definition of leadership and don't know what it truly means to lead.

All these years later, I realize that when I took that first job in the leadership development program at that large corporation, I failed to do something important: I neglected to ask employees of the company how they defined leadership. Without a definition, I couldn't evaluate what they valued or whether what they said aligned with how they behaved. I had fewer guidelines to determine whether the company at large aligned with my concept of leadership and my own values. And that meant that when the proverbial "leadershit" hit the fan, I was caught by surprise.

Sorting Through the Wreckage

Consider the last time you drove past the aftermath of a car accident. You may have slowed down, not just to accommodate the flow of traffic but also to check out the damage—dents, dangling mirrors, and, perhaps, worse. We stop to look on in awe when we encounter an accident. Do we heed the same wonder when people are driving beautifully?

Stories of disaster and devastation grab our attention. Often, our primitive nature is at work, attempting to keep us safe. Also, disaster unfortunately sells. Accounts of how well things are working? Not so much. It's one of those cruddy plights of being human, and our conceptions of leadership are not exempt. As a society, we are more likely notice the power-hungry, greedy, and charlatan tyrants than the truly grounded, humble leaders. We tend to take great, ethical, and service-oriented leaders for granted, often appreciating them only once we've lost them, not when they're still at the helm. We often recognize their traits in retrospect, especially when we come across a less effective or toxic leader thereafter.

A toxic relationship, with a leader or with anyone, is one in which the more you invest in that relationship, the worse it seemingly gets. And the only one seen as responsible for the relationship not working is you. On the contrary, a healthy relationship, with a leader or anyone, is one in which the more you invest in that relationship, the better it gets. And both people take responsibility for the relationship. Speak-up relationships are healthy relationships.

Fortunately, we can turn to those who have studied and practiced leadership at length and with great stakes for further insight, such as my dear friend and colleague, retired Navy SEAL Commander Rich Diviney.

Leader vs. Driver

In his book, *The Attributes: 25 Hidden Drivers of Optimal Performance,* Diviney notes that during his military career, he learned that "when it comes to being in charge, there are generally two kinds of people: drivers and leaders." What follows is, in my opinion, one of the greatest distinctions I've ever read on the topic:

> Drivers see their organization or team as a mechanical system, and they consider the people they're in charge of to be parts—buttons to push, levers to pull, pedals to press. Because they believe their vision is the most important one or the only valid one, they exert control through heavy handed direction and overt manipulation, sometimes with rewards but more often with punishments. If one of those parts doesn't perform as demanded, it's replaced without a second thought.

And, as Diviney explains, "there is no empathy because parts are expendable; no one mourns the worn-out brakes on their car."

No one chooses to follow a driver; they are pushed to, instead.

Meanwhile, leaders view their teams as living, breathing organisms (which, by the way, they are). As Diviney explains, "All types of leaders—parents and siblings; commanding officers and CEOs; presidents and priests; athletes and office managers—have one thing in common: They inspire."

"Inspire" comes from the Latin word *inspirare*, meaning "to breathe life into." Leaders literally breathe life into others, not just by what they say but especially by what they do. As Diviney shares, "Leaders aren't born. Leaders aren't made. Leaders are chosen based upon the way they behave." Leadership has nothing to do with title and everything to do with behavior. Leaders are purveyors of trust. As a result, "people follow leaders willingly, eagerly, because leaders motivate and influence. They might instruct but they do not dictate, encourage but not manipulate. People perform at their best for leaders not because they were ordered to but because they want to."

Think back to those who have moved you to action and those who have shoved you toward it, and you can clearly see the disparity between leaders and drivers.

Skills and Attributes

For more insight on how to define leadership, we can look to another distinction Diviney makes, one that serves as the central thesis of his book: the difference between skills and attributes.

Skills aren't inherent to our nature. They are learned and can be taught. Walking, talking, typing, and riding a bike all fall into the skills bucket. We aren't born with these abilities, though we can learn them. Skills are much more tactile, and thus easier to test, measure, and assess.

Meanwhile, attributes are inherent to our nature. They're there from the start. Think resilience, patience, adaptability, empathy, ambition, and so on. You can learn more about the attributes for optimal team performance in Diviney's book. If you have children, you'll notice some of their distinct attributes at a very young age. While we all have different levels of these attributes and they can be hard to see—they are the *intangibles*, if you will—we can develop them with intentional awareness, self-motivation, and deliberate effort.

On the one hand, as it turns out, listening is a skill. We can enroll in a two-hour class on how to be better listeners and emerge with the skills to do so. Compassion, on the other hand, is an attribute. There is no class we can take that will make us more compassionate. We must first see the merits of acting with compassion and then deliberately put ourselves in situations that enable that muscle to grow. As an aside, because compassion is an attribute, I felt compelled to include the word "truly" in front of "listen" in the subtitle of this book. Listening without compassion can quickly turn into manipulation.

Diviney realized the difference between skills and attributes during his Navy SEAL career as he headed training, selection, and assessment for an elite SEAL team. He found that they were turning down some of the strongest and most skilled candidates out there, but he had trouble articulating why.

During Basic Underwater Demolition/SEAL training, (BUD/S), candidates are tasked with swimming two lengths of a twenty-five-meter pool. Strong swimming skills are essential for SEALs, because they go where the enemy is most uncomfortable: the water, often at night (it's why we call them SEALs).

An apparently true story goes that when it was his turn, one trainee jumped into the water feet first, sunk to the bottom like a rock, and walked from one end of the pool to the other. Everyone thought this young sailor was nuts. By the time he had finished walking back to the other end, he had nearly drowned. As they yanked him back atop the pool deck, the instructor asked the trainee, "What the heck are you doing?!"

The young sailor answered, "Sir, I don't know how to swim."

"Oh," said the instructor, "we can teach you how to swim."

As it turned out, skills alone did not make a good SEAL—swimming, climbing, shooting, jumping out of airplanes, and so on could be taught. But their attributes were essential. The fact that this trainee didn't know how to swim did not stop him; he simply walked through the water, dangerous or not. He displayed the right attributes to make it.

Diviney began to identify the traits that made a good SEAL: It wasn't about brute and brawn. Those who made the cut were committed to the success and well-being of their fellow SEALs even more than their own welfare. They were biased toward service. They employed humor, making jokes when the going got tough, rather than throwing up their hands and quitting. (Indeed, retired SEALs mostly miss the laughter, joking, and camaraderie that formed while they served.) A good SEAL considered how to circumvent the rules to get what they and the team needed, as the non-swimmer displayed. Diviney calls this "cunning." These were *attributes*, not skills. They were hard-wired and could be developed—and that set those who had them up for greater success. When the going got tough, those attributes helped individuals and teams perform optimally. Having identified these attributes, Diviney and his team designed their selection and training programs to assess them along with skills.

Diviney realized, too, that while there are some skills that make good leaders, certain attributes make the best leaders. He identifies those as:

- **Empathy** (feeling with others)

- **Selflessness** (placing the needs and well-being of others ahead of one's own, despite a real or perceived risk)

- **Authenticity** (acting consistently with one's values, despite external pressures)

- **Decisiveness** (making decisions quickly and effectively)

- **Accountability** (taking ownership of one's decisions, actions, and the consequences thereof)

All these attributes make leaders supportive of those for whom they are responsible.

Leadership is not about status or title. We have all met, seen, or experienced "titles" who do not lead. Conversely, we have also experienced people who have no title or little authority yet behave as leaders. Leadership is in our behavior. To lead is a verb.

Leaders go first—they listen first, extend trust first, and courageously venture into the unknown first. Leaders put people and a cause ahead of profits and themselves. Leaders serve. Leaders show and act with care, empathy, and compassion. Leaders truly listen. They are consistent. Leaders give credit when things go right and take responsibility when things go wrong.

The only requisite of leadership is followership—whether others are ready and willing to follow you to where you're pointing and going. We follow those who lead, not for them but for ourselves. We follow those who lead because we feel as though they have our best interests at heart and in mind. We follow those who lead because they earn our trust through their behavior.

Know Thyself

So, how do people hone the innate attributes and learned skills necessary to thrive in a leadership role? That starts with the person they spend the most time with—I'm talking about the one in the mirror. Themselves.

I've taken part in countless leadership development programs over the course of my career, both as a participant and facilitator, and I've noticed a trend: every program I know of begins with a module on self-awareness and leading oneself. Great leaders are obsessed with building deeper relationships with their own attributes and skills, the people around them, and the world at large. Why?

We must do a tremendous amount of work to understand our own instrument before we can effectively help others tune and play theirs. This work is infinite in nature—it's never done. We can always learn more about ourselves, apply that knowledge, and help others do the same.

A great irony is that we can often be blind to our own strengths. Again, our own perception is our truth. We usually take for granted what we're world-class at, thinking that everyone walks around with the same strengths as we have. I'll give you an example.

My top strength is communication—I love finding words to match our ideas and emotions. As such, I will often draft emails, text messages, social media posts, and other content and ideas in my head as I let my mind wander, driving in the car or walking about. Sometimes I'll even pull over to write notes to capture an idea before it fades away. When I first revealed this to close friends not so long ago, I was shocked to hear that they didn't do the same. *Isn't everyone like me?!* Turns out not. We each have our own superhuman magic tricks, and we often downplay them and take them for granted. This is the reason assessments like StrengthsFinder, Sparketype, DISC, and many others are so valuable as personal, leadership, and team development tools.

It serves to understand your strengths, limitations, and gaps before you provide valuable—and credible—notes on those of others'. You must be secure enough in who you are to effectively talk about your strengths and admit your limitations with your team. Are you great at waxing philosophically but less so at execution (like I am)? That may mean that leveling with your team about how details and organization are not your strongest suits is wise and in order. If, when the going gets tough or feedback is provided, you tend to retreat, turn inward, and become pensive at first rather than springing to action, don't leave it up to your team to guess what's going on. Let them know! Share your preferences and tendencies so you can best communicate, understand, team up, and weather any storms together.

When you can be honest about why and how you show up the way you do, demonstrating the leadership necessary to get things done and the vulnerability to admit where and why you need support, those elements become embedded in your culture. That leadership and vulnerability is positively contagious: it can inspire others to learn about and share more about themselves, too, with the benefit of the team thriving.

"Vulnerability" is not just a nice word—it's a leadership imperative for building trusting, sustainably high-performing teams. Vulnerability means you display the courage to wear both your limitations and your strengths on your sleeve. When you and your team know one another's strengths, weaknesses, and gaps, you're far better attuned to know who should step up and lead, who should support, and who should step back. And this approach isn't static. It is constantly, dynamically evolving based on what is emerging in the present. Vulnerability is also not about sharing all things, all the time, and with all people. That could simply be oversharing—not everything is suitable for work, and we ought to be mindful of what we're sharing, when we're sharing it, and with whom.

This is what appropriate vulnerability can look like:

> Hey team, I'm struggling with a family health matter. I will likely be short on sleep for the next couple of weeks. I'll keep you posted as things develop. I see work as a bit of a refuge and distraction from some of the things going on, so please don't ask me about it. If I want your support, I'll let you know, and if I seem foggy or distracted, that's probably why, and I simply ask for a bit of extra grace and space right now. Thank you.

While everyone will individually deal a little differently with a matter like this, the takeaway of the above example is to set an expectation and boundaries, which could shift if the issue persists for a longer period.

Conversely, a senior leader sharing out of the blue with all employees that the company is out of money is not radical vulnerability, that's radical irresponsibility. Appropriate vulnerability could be going to the board, colleagues, or a peer network ahead of the issue becoming a catastrophe, then enlisting a team to solve matters ahead.

For vulnerability to work as the superpower it is, context is key. When we share appropriately with our teams, we can best support one another, take charge, and rally together.

Leadership is about owning our impact on others, even if that impact was unintended.

Closing the Say-Do Gap

Another important benefit comes from getting to know oneself: closing the say-do gap.

Although we are considering a standard definition for leadership, there is no uniform way to lead. There must be room for nuance, context, and subtleties, just as is the case with most things in our human experience. Leadership isn't uniform. Leadership is personal. The real question is whether as a leader you do what you say, and own up to it when, not if, you miss the mark.

Most leaders and organizations *say* the right things. But just because they say they value something doesn't mean they live it. The truly great leaders walk their talk, especially when the going gets tough. For instance, had I asked, my first employer may have provided a definition of leadership that aligned with my own—one that spoke to the importance of empathy, compassion, selflessness, service, authenticity, decisiveness, and accountability. But after some time working there, I would have perceived that the organization's true definition of leadership was tied to title, authority, and profit and loss—performance above all else.

As the saying goes, actions speak far louder than words. If leaders and organizations have a say-do gap, the truth will come out, and it will be represented in the culture and results.

Of course, nobody's perfect. None of us does exactly what we say all the time. But we can do our best, attempting to own and clean up our messes, apologizing when we screw up, and always trying to improve. Leadership is about owning our impact on others even if that impact was unintended.

The greatest leaders stay great in large part because of the people they surround themselves with. In fact, the power leaders inherit can cause them to act as if they've "suffered a traumatic brain injury—becoming more impulsive, less risk-aware, and, crucially, less adept at seeing things from other people's point of view." Under the influence of power, leaders can experience an empathy deficit, according to UC Berkeley psychology professor Dacher Keltner. This leads to a "power paradox": once a leader has power, they lose some of the capacities they needed to gain it in the first place. As we'll explore further in chapter 9, an antidote to this power intoxication is to welcome candor with care—feedback from trusted partners, advisors, and friends to ground us in our humanity. As when Michelle Obama reminds her husband and his followers that indeed his feet smell like the rest of ours.

Drivers and narcissists tend to surround themselves with "yes people"—after all, a narcissist's own opinion is the most valid. Great and humble leaders foster a speak-up culture, surrounding themselves with people who dish them their truth—their ideas, concerns, disagreements, and mistakes. Great leaders listen, act . . . and change their socks.

The Best Leaders Develop More Leaders

In addition to knowing ourselves as best we can, and leading others in a manner that works for them and the team (remember that Platinum Rule we introduced in chapter 3), we have another crucial responsibility: equipping others to take on leadership responsibilities. Kendra Reddy, an executive coach, keynote speaker, and writer, playfully calls it being a "leader breeder." And in many ways, it is the true test of leadership: Can you teach and support others as they wish to lead, to care for those in *their* span? No matter how great we are at leading, the true test of our leadership is in our ability to help others become great leaders, who then help others become great leaders. You get the point. And the goal is not to replicate yourself. The goal is to help others discover what makes them world-class and then help them become it.

Perhaps landing on an entirely universal definition of leadership isn't possible, or necessary. After all, there are no hard-and-fast rules when it comes to human dynamics—what works for me won't necessarily work for you. But we can identify the basic responsibilities of a leader: to understand oneself, to care for others as they want to be cared for, and to contribute to the growth of others who choose to take up that same call to lead. Leaders constantly take themselves on to examine and close their own say-do gap and they consistently develop their leadership attributes.

In the context of our teams and organizations, we owe it to ourselves and others to define what we mean by leadership, to be true to the values that we, as individuals and as organizations, espouse. With a clear definition of what leadership means in a particular team, organization, or context, we can better select, promote, and train based on that definition. Without that kind of clarity and alignment, you're at risk of getting "leadershit"— drivers who prioritize results rather than people, at all costs. But with a solid understanding of the job description of leadership— both in general and at your organization in particular—and a good strategy for selection, you can put the right people in the right seats for leaders, teams, and organizations to thrive. And to that I say, giddy on up!

5

Select Better Leaders

"Who you are surrounded by often determines who you become."

VICKI SAUNDERS

FIRST MET Andrew Corner when he was leading logistics operations in Europe for a top global brand—one we all know. As we toured the company's state-of-the-art buildings— where some five thousand employees worked under his supervision—he turned to me, gestured to the many people on the shop floor, and said, "I can't do their jobs."

While others might wonder how he could lead a whole lot of people with tasks he couldn't tackle himself, it made perfect sense to me. A leader doesn't need to know how to do everyone's job. That's not their role. Their role is to listen, care, remove obstacles, make decisions when necessary, give credit often, take responsibility (especially when things don't go well), and support their people, among other actions.

I recently heard a senior marketing leader at the same company say, "If I'm the best marketer in the room, we have a problem. My role is to find, support, and create the conditions for the people around me to bring their greatest talents, gifts, knowledge, and genius to the forefront." That's the goal of leadership—to raise others up and help them shine.

Corner embodies this approach. He realizes that leadership is not about catching more fish; it's about teaching and supporting people to catch fish in their own way. The most logical choice then is to trust that his team knows what they need to do their jobs best, to empower them, and to build a speak-up culture in which they will ask for what they need along the way. This ethos of empowerment helps make him a great leader.

Where Selection Goes Wrong

Most organizations take a different tack. Rather than appointing a leader who is focused on best equipping team members to excel in their jobs, promotions into leadership positions often use performance as a primary metric. Leaders are brought on because of their exceptional ability to perform the work itself. Those called up are typically the most driven, high-performing, talented, and, often, charismatic or extroverted of the bunch. These characteristics aren't bad, but the work of leadership additionally requires a service orientation.

Adding to the challenge of leadership, new leaders are often put in charge of the people who were, a day before, their peers and friends. The dynamics of that relationship change, and we don't support leaders well enough into this transition.

How many people turn down a promotion? People typically accept promotions—and the pay, status, and responsibility that comes with them—even if they're not necessarily interested or equipped in the leadership aspect of the position. If you want to be in a position of leadership for the perks, your own ego, or because that's the next thing you should do, do us a favor and *don't* do it. If you want to be a leader to serve, sacrifice, and improve the well-being of the people and world around you, well then, green light!

As an aside, some of the best leaders I've met and most admire are introverts. On the one hand, extroverts (like me) can get themselves into trouble because they're more likely to enjoy and gain energy from the spotlight. Am I speaking up to serve or am I speaking up to be seen, admired, and energized? Introverts, on the other hand, may be less comfortable and expend greater energy in that spotlight. When an introvert feels called to step up, step out, and lead, it usually means they feel a strong connection to something bigger than themselves that matters. *Well, someone should do something about this! Shucks, I guess I'm someone.*

I do know one leader who turned down a promotion because, as it turns out, not all promotions are created equal. About a year into the COVID-19 pandemic, the Great Resignation was raging. The economics of employment began to sway in favor of employees. People were leaving their jobs, or changing jobs, in droves.

Hannah was an up-and-comer. She had risen the ranks in her career and was now working as a senior director inside a huge multinational organization. In late summer 2021, she received an email from her boss, a senior vice president, with the following message:

> As you know, several people have left their roles, many at your level. To retain your employment at this organization we'd like to offer you a promotion to a Vice President (VP) level.
>
> Please find a PDF attached with the VP positions that are available. Select which role you would like and respond to your respective chief executive within five business days.

The attached PDF simply listed titles and had no further description. Hannah thought to herself, *Nope, that's not how this is going to go.* She had the courage to reply to her boss that this was the not the way she was going to get promoted to VP. Hannah cares deeply about using her strengths to solve meaningful challenges and create meaningful opportunities. She wanted to know more about what she was saying yes to, to set everyone up to thrive—the company included. She also didn't want to abandon the amazing team she was currently leading. Her boss informed her that her decision would not be a popular response with her chief executive, to which Hannah responded, "I'll let them know myself because this is the type of behavior that is causing my peers to flee this organization." Boom. Mic drop.

Hannah met with her C-suite leader and shared her feedback diplomatically, which, to the senior leader's credit, was received extremely well and with humility. Funny how senior leaders can be so removed and shielded from the truth of the impact of their decisions or behavior. Hannah then spent the next number of months, in partnership with other leaders and HR, exploring what role would be ideal. She received her promotion, and she displayed the courage to ensure she received it in a way that would set her, those around her, and the company up for success. Everyone won. She and her new team are now thriving.

We are a hierarchical species, so leadership roles come with increased status, which can be desirable. The issue is that the types of "leaders" who care most about rank, status, and power often make the most toxic leaders. We ought to embrace leadership as what it should be and is—a responsibility and a service to be given. When leaders show up to care and serve, their people perform better and their well-being increases, which benefits them, their teams, and their relationships outside work. Leaders earn followers, engagement, discretionary effort, and loyalty as their reward.

Frans de Waal studies the social behavior of primates—how they fight and reconcile, share, and cooperate. He's discovered fascinating parallels between how humans and primates choose their best leaders. Studying chimpanzees, de Waal found that both chimps and humans are dominance-hierarchical and power hungry. In chimpanzees, the "alphas" are not necessarily the strongest. The longest-lasting, most popular, and most successful leaders do not behave as bullies. The most successful alphas are the most cooperative, generous, and empathetic of the group. These alphas keep the peace, provide comfort, and stabilize the group. This behavior is not solely service-oriented or altruistic, however. These alphas act this way for the benefits of popularity, respect, and staying in power. Unfortunately, we humans have adopted the term "alpha" typically to denote overly aggressive, bullying behavior, rather than the true leadership behavior that is far more nurturing in virtually all primates.

So, how do we ensure that we select the right leaders and cultivate the ideal leadership behaviors in them?

There's a whole lot of opportunity to select better leaders. For example, what if we used leadership criteria instead of primarily focusing on performance for selection? What if we instituted 360-degree peer reviews as part of the hiring and promotion process, enabling people to have a say in who their leaders will be? After all, wouldn't you work harder for someone you helped choose?

Navy SEAL Trust and Performance Matrix

We can again look to Rich Diviney and the Navy SEALs for insight on identifying those up for the job of leadership.

The Navy SEALs are among the highest-performing teams operating amid the hardest-to-perform conditions of all time, and the stakes are high: life and death, fate of foreign relations.

That leaves little to no room for error when it comes to leadership selection.

In *The Attributes*, Diviney shares a story from his basic training days that he reflected on when considering his team selection criteria: One day in SEAL training, he and his fellow trainees were on the beach in Coronado, California, undergoing what used to be called "surf torture." It's now called "surf conditioning"—more politically correct, I guess. The SEAL trainees were lying at the edge of the water as frigid Pacific Ocean waves rushed up and cascaded over them time after time. Meanwhile, the instructors running the exercise walked along the line of potential SEALs with a megaphone, announcing, "Anyone who wants to quit, we got hot coffee and doughnuts."

The guy next to Diviney quipped, "You got any chocolate glazed ones? Because I ain't quitting unless you got chocolate glazed!" Diviney and this jokester shared in a laugh because it was funny. The man on the other side of Diviney did not so much as crack a smile. He was too lost in his own head, pain, and discomfort. At that moment, Diviney knew that he and the jokester would get through the gruesome exercise, though he doubted his other neighbor's fate. Sure enough, minutes later, their frigid neighbor "rang the bell" and quit both the exercise and SEAL training altogether. Diviney and his neighbor who instigated the laughter made it through.

This is the reason Diviney values humor as a great attribute for what he calls "teamability." Laughter releases a trifecta of neurochemicals that served Diviney and his surf mate during that trying exercise. It can serve anyone in challenging times. Laughter releases dopamine (*this is good, keep going*), endorphins (*this doesn't hurt so much*), and oxytocin (*we're in this together*). Creating and finding the funny makes hard things easier to get through.

Diviney began to see that skills (knowing how to do the job) and attributes (how you interact with your team) seemed to fall on a matrix. You'll remember that skills can be taught and attributes are innate, though they can be developed. It's why the SEALs chose the trainee who couldn't swim and instead decided to walk along the bottom of the pool to complete the challenge in front of them. You can teach someone how to swim, but you can't necessarily school them on how to take a risk, have a sense of humor, or show up for their teammates. Ultimately, attributes more strongly determine a person's trustworthiness—an essential element in any team environment. And so was born the Navy SEAL Trust-Performance Matrix, made popular by Simon Sinek. The value of this matrix extends to anyone looking to select and promote great leaders and teammates.

Navy SEAL Trust-Performance Matrix

HIGH PERFORMANCE LOW TRUST	HIGH PERFORMANCE MEDIUM TRUST	HIGH PERFORMANCE HIGH TRUST
MEDIUM PERFORMANCE LOW TRUST	MEDIUM PERFORMANCE MEDIUM TRUST	MEDIUM PERFORMANCE HIGH TRUST
LOW PERFORMANCE LOW TRUST	LOW PERFORMANCE MEDIUM TRUST	LOW PERFORMANCE HIGH TRUST

PERFORMANCE

TRUST

Of course, we all want to hire and promote people who are high performers and trustworthy—the upper right corner of the matrix. But when we must decide between performance and trustworthiness, someone who is low performance but high on trust is the better pick. The extremely high-performing SEALs would pick a lower performer of high trust ten times out of ten. Countless studies and firsthand accounts from virtually everyone I've worked with over the course of my career demonstrate that those who rank high on performance but low on trust are destructive to any work environment. On the flip side, someone whose behavior generates trust earned from those around them is probably worth the risk and investment, even if they're presently underperforming or may not possess the perfect match of skills for a role. As Diviney teaches us, skills measure what is, while attributes determine potential—what could be.

Look no further than a team's answers to "who is the jerk?" or "who is in it for themselves?" to reveal the high performer of low trust (and, if you don't know the answer, either you have high trust throughout your team . . . or you might be the problem!). I believe there is a strong correlation between being a high performer of low trust and being a driver. While the high performer of low trust may perform well in front of a client or in a boardroom full of superiors, they tend to be awful to work with behind the scenes. They may get the job done in the short term, but they throw a destructive wake behind them. Rating higher on trust, regardless of rank on performance, suggests someone who will create safe relationships where teammates can grow together.

For example, when we're hiring an accountant, we look for someone with a specific skill set. I wouldn't recommend an accountant who cannot read a balance sheet. However, a person doesn't need to be *the best* at reading balance sheets to be an effective accountant, teammate, and, especially, leader. The Trust-Performance Matrix can help us approach selecting for all roles with a greater awareness of the optimal attributes for leadership and teamability.

Many of us have surely been in the hiring situation in which one candidate is the best match on paper—their résumé checks every box, from experiences to education—but another candidate, who stacks up not nearly as well on paper, seems as if they would add much more to the team dynamic and results. Typically, the wisest choice is the lesser-qualified candidate who will be a more beneficial addition to the team. Even the dreamiest of dream teams is doomed if there isn't the right mix of attitudes and attributes. Dream teams composed of the most talented individuals may perform well when everything is smooth sailing, but the true test of a team is how they manage and perform in times of challenge, stress, and uncertainty. When trouble hits a team where trust is low, they're likely to enter an "every-person-for-themselves" game of survival.

Teams composed of consistent, essential, and complementary attributes can weather the greatest of storms. Adversity brings high-trust teams closer together—and they perform better through challenge, stress, and uncertainty time and again.

Certain innate ways of being make some people better suited than others for specific roles. But if you're a senior leader, you're not always best positioned to determine a person's attributes, particularly when it comes to trust.

There's Always More to the Story

The more senior you are in an organization, the further you may be from the truth. This makes it even more important to gain from perspectives other than your own: those of your peers, and those more junior when it comes to hiring, selection, and promotion.

I once had a direct report whom I very much enjoyed working with. I knew she had a lot on her plate, both professionally and personally, but she always brought what I thought was her best to the table. I trusted her. Turns out, I was being played.

Not long into her tenure, complaints about her began to roll in from the rest of my team. Numerous people reported having very different interactions with her than the kind I was having. They mentioned issues with her attitude, performance, and even her ethics. I realized I had to get to the bottom of things.

When she and I sat down to discuss the other team members' feedback, she denied it all. The conversation was seemingly going nowhere, and I sensed that she wasn't being forthright with me. I took a risk and shared, "I care for you. I respect you. I love working with you. I also care for, respect, and love working with the other members of our team. I have a problem because you're denying the feedback that all the other people on the team are sharing with me about you. Help me reconcile this."

After I said that, she came clean, and from that point, we were better able to move forward productively.

Here's the moral of the story: When you are in a position of authority, some people may suck up to you to stay in good standing, get what they want, or simply keep their job. That means, as a leader, you won't always have a true and holistic sense of what's going on. Not all voices are of the same quality, regardless of their volume. Sucking up is not the same as speaking up. We may defer to those in power out of respect, intimidation, or fear. As a result, a leader's truth is not necessarily the whole truth. It is but one perspective.

For a fuller picture, this equation can shift your mindset:

Your Truth + My Truth = Higher Truth

You must take time to gain from the perspectives of others to see what's truly going on. Trust your gut, of course, but don't stop there. You won't know if your instincts are spot-on, way off, or just scratching the surface until you consistently survey others. And when you do, you must listen and act accordingly if you want to keep hearing their truth. Remember, make it safe and make it worth it.

In our cultures,
**we get the behavior
we reward and the
behavior we tolerate.**

Beware of Who and What You Reward

In our cultures, we get the behavior we reward and the behavior we tolerate. Indeed, tolerating behavior is a form of accepting and rewarding it. If we reward or tolerate those who are high on performance but low on trust—those who kiss up to the higher-ups while treating their peers and subordinates poorly— they will prevail. The environment and every member of their team will suffer.

A multinational tech company took this insight to heart. The company was known for its excellent culture, leadership development initiatives, and employee retention. The leadership team put in the work to keep it that way. They evaluate leaders in a twofold manner: 50 percent on their performance-based contributions and 50 percent on their contributions to company culture. One leader, a VP at the company, shared with me that she was among the top performers in the business, generating impressive results. But her culture scores were among the lowest of her peers. When the results came in, the senior leadership team took them seriously and acted.

They told the VP that she could keep a job with the company but she would be demoted to an individual contributor role and required to re-enroll in the company's leadership development program. If she learned to understand the value of culture and put in the work to bolster it, she could earn her VP role again.

The company also introduced more frequent pulse and micro-surveys, no longer wanting to rely on an annual survey and review system as the company continued to grow.

This story has a happy ending. The former VP went through the leadership program for a second time, understood the error of her ways, and developed the perspective and strategies necessary to contribute earnestly to the company's culture. She re-earned her title two years later, and her culture *and* performance scores improved. The company's commitment to culture—and the VP's willingness to grow—resulted in a better outcome for all.

Selecting Better

But how do you hire and promote better in the first place, particularly when some can fake their leadership and cultural fit in a forty-five-minute interview? Some people may not be great in the role; they're simply great at interviewing for the role. The question is, how do you conduct interviews in a way that measures not just skills but attributes?

When my sister was interviewing for medical school, she encountered a particularly interesting technique. The Michael G. DeGroote School of Medicine in Hamilton, Ontario, has been known for producing excellent family medicine practitioners. (Admittedly, I'm a little biased.)

Family doctors see it all. To be effective, they should be able to help people of all ages and at all stages, which requires them to think on their feet and communicate complex concepts in simple ways. As such, the medical school highly values effective communication, care, and patience (a good bedside manner), humility, and even creativity in their prospective medical school candidates.

With all that in mind, my sister found herself in front of a panel of three interviewers as one of her final steps in the admissions process. Toward the end of a full day of interviews, tours, and activities, one of the panelists prompted my sister, out of the blue, with a request: "Teach us something you're passionate about."

Why did they pose such a question without giving her any time to prepare? The best time to see attributes in action—

someone's true colors—is when you expose them to stress, uncertainty, and challenge.

My sister gathered her thoughts; this certainly wasn't in any of the prep books.

"Well," she said, "I love to dance. I'll teach you the first dance steps I ever learned . . ." She asked the members of the panel to stand up and she began to teach them basic ballet: first position, second position, and so on . . .

She demonstrated that she could teach others and communicate something new and complex in a simple way. She showed that she could accept the challenge with humility and exude care, patience, and understanding as she did so (the interview panel members' dance abilities were quite suspect). They weren't evaluating her on her ability to make them better ballet dancers. They were examining her ability to think on her feet (quite literally) and to communicate with ease, calm, clarity, and grace.

Today, my sister is a great family physician (and while I am biased, fortunately reviews on the Rate MDs website agree!). Take a cue from my sister's medical school admissions committee and throw your candidates some strategic and telling curveballs. Expose them to the types of stress, uncertainty, and challenges they'll rightfully experience on the job, and see how they respond.

If you're hiring a sales professional, you could send them a package with information a week ahead of their interview, letting them know they'll have thirty minutes to pitch a particular product and lead a mock sales meeting. Certainly, evaluate their performance on this. When they complete that exercise at the interview, let them know that they'll now have two minutes to prepare to sell you a product sitting on the table—a pencil, or a whiteboard, or anything unexpected and obscure—and see how they respond. Are they humble? Are they funny? Do they seem to act like a victim, or do they rise to the challenge? As you observe them, you're no longer evaluating them on their performance, because it will likely be ugly. You must evaluate their behavior and how they might respond in a similar situation on the job.

Or you could throw out the formal environment altogether and conduct one of your interviews in an escape room (you can learn a lot about a person in an escape room). If teamwork and solving problems together as a team is essential for the role they're interviewing for, how they perform as an individual contributor and teammate in an escape room would be telling. Or take them to a restaurant and observe how they treat the waitstaff. You could even slip the waitstaff a twenty-dollar bill to purposefully mess up their order to see how they respond— with respect or tact? Are they rude and dismissive? Or do they shrink, become meek, and not mention anything at all? There is no right answer but depending on your culture and what you're looking for in a particular role, any of these exercises could prove quite revealing and valuable. When you switch things up—particularly on the fly—you'll learn a lot about how people lead and who they truly are. It's also kind of fun.

A client of mine did just that. They were hiring for a role that required the individual to have a mix of skills and attributes, namely, being highly organized, detail-oriented, and responsible. So, at the end of a promising virtual video interview, the interviewer asked the candidate, "Are you highly organized, detail-oriented, and responsible?"

"Why, yes!" the interviewee proudly (and meaninglessly) exclaimed.

"Well," the interviewer responded, "prove it."

The interviewee thought for a moment. And then, *eureka!* "I just organized my cutlery bin," she said. "Would you like to see it?"

"Absolutely," the interviewer said.

The candidate brought her laptop into her kitchen and tilted the camera so her interviewer could see the drawer. Indeed, it was perfectly organized and spotless, and they could hear the pride in her voice and demeanor as she described her cleaning and organizing methodology. She got the job and has been an amazing addition to the team since her first day.

Selecting and promoting those who are up for the job of leadership can be a make or break between people wanting to show up to work or avoiding their boss at all costs. Again, leadership either feeds or depletes. When we understand what makes a great teammate and leader, and how to identify those attributes in people, we're better positioned to hire and promote the people who will make a real, positive difference for our teams, organizations, and results. The next step is to ensure we're supporting them as best we can once they are in the role, or even ahead of it, so they can excel in what we've tasked them with.

6

Help Leaders Lead

*"Everything I learned about parenting
is leadership and everything I learned
about leadership was wrong."*

BOB CHAPMAN

ALWAYS KNEW I wanted to be a parent. As the youngest kid of three, for as long as I can remember, I assumed growing a family of my own was a given. As an adult, I was lucky enough for circumstances, like having a great life partner, to align to make it so. When my amazing wife, Julie, and I felt ready *enough*, we went for it. Fortunately, it happened for us—twice!

For some, the decision to become a parent is a deliberate and slow one. For others, it can be quick—sometimes not so well thought out, or not a decision at all. Some people try and it doesn't go to plan, so they seek alternate means. Others have no interest in it and go out of their way to ensure it doesn't happen. Regardless, if you do get the job and awesome responsibility of being a parent, the choice *to have* a child is very different from *raising* a child.

The same goes for leadership. The decision to seek out and accept a promotion or otherwise step into a leadership role can be simple and straightforward. The act of leading and supporting your people consistently is a different decision and responsibility altogether.

While my wife and I felt we were prepared for the role of parenting, we weren't. I think this is a common feeling among first-time parents (and leaders). For example, before becoming a parent, I thought I was quite a patient person. But our children have proved me otherwise. Unbeknownst to me, I had (and still have) much work to do to grow and flex my patience muscles. That work has helped both in my parenting and in my leadership responsibilities. But there isn't much that can truly prepare you for parenting—or leadership—quite like being on the job.

We might easily judge a leader's moves when we're not in their shoes. Often, it's only when we take on a leadership role ourselves that we realize the challenges and monumental mountains that those who led us were scaling all along. And unfortunately—as is the case with parenting—there's never quite enough we can do to prepare for leadership until we're on duty. Worse, when we take on a leadership or managerial role, it's often years before we receive any formal training at all. Not a great recipe for success.

The Leadership Training Gap

I remember bringing our firstborn, our daughter, home from the hospital. Julie and I were somewhat clueless, and the mind-melting exhaustion from labor and delivery (okay, my wife pulled all the weight there) and a few near-sleepless nights in hospital only added to our unease and disorientation. Even though we knew we'd make mistakes, our main motivation in those early days was not to break our baby or mess her up too badly. On our drive back home—now a family of three—we desperately called for reinforcements, tagging in my sister and brother-in-law (who were a year ahead of us as young parents themselves) to watch our baby daughter for a couple hours while Julie and I caught some winks and attempted to recover some semblance of sanity. (They also brought us the best Italian takeout this palate has ever tasted. I think circumstances played with my tastebuds on that one.)

New leaders often find themselves in a similar uneasy and disorienting position (perhaps, though, without the Italian takeout). In 2012, leadership development consultant Jack Zenger wanted to find the answer to this question: "When do managers first get leadership training?" Zenger and his team examined a database of global leaders who had taken part in their training—around seventeen thousand leaders in virtually every sector. They found that the average age of the participants in their programs was forty-two. However, the average age of supervisors at these same firms was thirty-three, and typically, they took on a supervisory role for the first time at age thirty. That meant many leaders weren't receiving any leadership training until they had been in a leadership position for more than a decade. As Zenger explains, "Practicing anything mildly important . . . without training is inadvisable. The fact that so many of your managers are practicing leadership without training should alarm you."

It seems obvious, but let's dig in further. Zenger describes what happens in the absence of training. For one, we can follow our sometimes-ill-advised intuition, pick up bad habits, and cobble together a haphazard approach to the challenge in front of us and continue applying it to the issues that come our way. Zenger likens it to a skier or golfer learning without initial instructions, making it up as they go. They form bad habits that become harder and harder to break the more they are reinforced. That means our potentially flawed thinking and strategies end up playing a role in every decision we make, possibly for years on end. Practice makes progress only if done correctly. If you're practicing your home-grown approach, you're not necessarily getting better at leadership, you're just becoming more practiced at whatever you've brought to the table to begin with.

"Supervisors are, of course, leading people from the first day on the job," Zenger says. "And from that day habits are being formed. Attitudes are being created. Management practices begin to coalesce. Would it not be in the organization's and individuals' best interest to begin that process the moment they're selected for that position?" Or maybe even before?

Zenger shares a question he's been asked throughout his career: "With all the money and effort being spent on leadership development programs, why don't we have better leaders?" While the response to that question is complex and multifaceted, could part of the answer be that we simply wait too long to teach leaders the skills and help them develop the attributes required? Should we not develop the people who are in the roles or aspire to lead as soon as we can?

This is particularly important in an organizational context in which we often promote people based on skills, performance results, who they know, and if we like them. In many cases, those who are taking on leadership positions haven't developed their leadership attributes—like empathy, selflessness, authenticity, decisiveness, and accountability—or been given the opportunity to do so, or even been told they're important. As a result, they may not have a strong sense of security in their own leadership, and—worse—they are likely not surrounded by many great leadership peers, mentors, and role models to call upon when they're unsure of how best to proceed.

Now, that doesn't mean you need to invest hundreds of thousands of dollars in formal leadership training. A leadership development program can start with something as simple as running a book club: pick a relevant book to study, unpack it, and bring its learnings and applications to life and to the job together in community.

Some of the greatest leadership development I have experienced in my career came in the form of extracurriculars. As a junior employee, I sought out and was given the opportunity to own part of the company's United Way fundraising campaign, and while the business stakes may have been relatively low, the practice was real. I've seen organizations do amazing things with hackathons, agile work sprints, and other activities that have real business impact. One of the greatest ways to support those who wish to lead is to give them meaningful experiences well before they are promoted to the formal roles.

Of course, any form of training or extracurricular can prepare us only so much (just ask anyone who's been in the trenches of new parenthood). Again, on-the-job training is often ideal. Doing right by those in your span of care means considering the shifting context. Parenting a newborn takes a different set of skills and attributes than it does a three-year-old, a thirteen-year-old, and a thirty-five-year-old, and ages in between and beyond. The same goes for leadership. Supporting our people is about more than just training. There is no one-size-fits-all approach. It's about meeting your team where they are, where they want to be met, where they wish to be led, and where the organization and team need to go. And it's about doing so with empathy.

Forget Gold, Go for Platinum!

Earlier, we covered the difference between the Golden Rule and the Platinum Rule: treating others as *we* want to be treated (Gold) versus treating others as *they* wish to be treated (Platinum). To lead others most effectively, we ought to focus on

Our job as a leader is to teach, guide, mentor, coach, and support, not to tell people how we did it and make them do it our way.

understanding not only what makes us tick but especially what makes others tick. After all, once we become leaders, our job is to teach, guide, mentor, coach, and support, not to tell people how we did it and make them do it our way. Our way may not be the best way, certainly isn't the only way, and likely isn't their way. Supporting others while practicing the Platinum Rule is hard work, and it requires an individualized approach—one we need to develop ourselves and in the leaders we lead. Although it takes effort and is hard to scale, it's well worth it.

We aren't mind readers, so how can we know how others wish to be led? Well, we can 1) observe, 2) ask them, and 3) ask others.

This may mean that when you welcome a new member to your team, you tell them a little bit about your style—how you like to lead and work with a team—and invite them to share some of their own preferences. Then you can open the door for future conversations, saying something like, "This isn't the only time we can have this discussion. We can always revisit, reflect, and adjust as we get to know each other better and as our relationship, the team, and the work continue to evolve." This isn't a one-time, static form to fill out. People ought to be allowed—encouraged—to say things like, "I'm not sure yet. Let me think about that and get back to you," "I changed my mind," or "I think I've learned more about myself."

I have seen team members create and share their own internal profiles among their teams, including their personal purpose, strengths, values, attributes, personality assessment results, hobbies, working hours, and so on. I've seen teams display them, physically posted in the office or on virtual boards, so anyone can access them at any time to learn more about their team members' preferences. This can be useful when planning meetings and events, approaching someone for a feedback conversation, planning to get them a gift, and more. You can make it a powerful team habit to practice the Platinum Rule.

Understanding others' preferences may mean shifting your approach and adjusting to the needs of others. I encourage you to check in and ask if you're getting it right, or what you could be doing better. Indeed, we aren't mind readers, or at least very good ones.

Put the Appreciation Languages to Work

There are also plenty of great tools and assessments out there to better understand yourself and others. StrengthsFinder, the Myers-Briggs Type Indicator, DiSC, Insights, Hogan assessments, Sparketype, the Four Tendencies Quiz, The Attributes assessments, and many more, including *The 5 Languages of Appreciation in the Workplace.*

Gary Chapman and Paul White have outlined five ways that we prefer to give and receive appreciation. The 5 Languages of Appreciation are:

- Acts of service
- Giving tangible gifts
- Appropriate physical touch
- Quality time
- Words of affirmation

Chapman and White hold that, while we value all the appreciation languages to some extent, each of us typically favors a primary appreciation language and a secondary one. That means we most prefer appreciation delivered in those forms and tend to prefer expressing appreciation to others in the same way—regardless of whether it's *their* appreciation language.

I had a very real experience of this, and it happened back on a familiar date—September 7, 2009. If you recall, this was day one at my first corporate gig out of university—the same date one thousand people were let go post-merger. Yikes. I had just finished my first job training session with my predecessor when the clock struck noon—everyone's favorite time of the workday—*lunch!* Well, perhaps second-favorite time.

We walked down to the corporate campus cafeteria. My new colleague and I grabbed our sandwiches, chose a spot to sit, and began to chat and chow down. Just as we started, a familiar person walked into the cafeteria. It was Abi—remember her? She was a member of the HR team and had been instrumental in my recruiting and preboarding journey. She was also the one who called me in March 2009 to reassure me I still had the job following the announced merger. I knew so few people at the company on that first day that a familiar face felt very assuring to me. She walked over to us to say hello, and I was so excited to see her that I stood up and gave her a hug. It felt appropriate. She had helped me get to this place in my career and I was grateful.

I felt the tension: it was as if my hug had transformed Abi into a wooden telephone pole. It was likely the worst hug of my life. After a short, awkward exchange, Abi moved along. My predecessor stared at me with his mouth slightly agape and said, "Dude, what did you just do?"

"What?"

"We don't hug here," he explained.

Oh, I thought to myself, *if they don't hug around here, I'm not sure I should be around here.*

Now, in many cases, physical touch is not appropriate in work contexts. Always seek consent before touching a colleague, whether that's a hug, a hand on the shoulder, or anything else. In some contexts, like in Montreal, Quebec, it is customary to greet colleagues with kisses on each cheek, while only two hours away, in Canada's capital city, Ottawa, kissing a colleague on the cheek would be completely inappropriate. So, custom, preferences, and the consent of others are important to be aware of.

Truthfully, I could have done a far better job in this situation with Abi.

Regardless, following the hug, the cultural dissonance had already commenced for me. Oh well. Better to find out early, I guess. Even better to find out before saying yes to the job offer. But, hey, I was young, inexperienced, and naive. This was my first job out of business school, and it was better to get *some* experience rather than none. This was a useful early-career lesson for me on the Platinum Rule: just because I was a hugger certainly didn't mean everyone was. This was a preference and a cultural nuance I should have known about and respected. Now, if hugging was so important to me or I believed more people ought to embrace the oxytocin benefits of a darn good hug, I may have chosen to eschew cultural convention, set a new trend, request to hug anyway, or self-select out of the culture to find a more hug-welcome zone.

A coaching client of mine also came to a Platinum Rule revelation during one of our sessions. He was but a few weeks into a new C-suite role when he mentioned wanting to reward and recognize one of his team members—his chief of staff—for going above and beyond. As he was new in this role and the organization, he had an aggressive agenda to get up to speed on the lay of the land. His chief of staff had been working extremely hard, stretching the boundaries of her capacity to keep up.

"I'm going to send her some flowers," he said.

"Does she like flowers?" I asked.

"I don't know," he said.

"Maybe you should find out first. Do you know anyone who would know?" I asked. He nodded.

Upon digging deeper, he might find that she didn't care much for flowers. Or that she'd much prefer chocolate. Or that gift-giving wasn't her appreciation language; words of affirmation were, and it would be much more meaningful to share his appreciation over the phone or via handwritten note. Or perhaps she'd like it best if he mentioned all she'd done in front of the whole team. Who knows? She does, and so will other colleagues and friends who know her well. Find out. Act in accordance. It will make a world of difference for others and feel pretty good for you to make a difference in recognizing others in the way most meaningful to them.

I told this story of personalized recognition to a friend who is the CEO and cofounder of a successful scale-up. He cofounded the company in 2016, and at the time of this writing, it had more than sixty employees. When I mentioned this flower anecdote to him, he exclaimed, "That's great, but I can't do that for all sixty-plus people at my company. I don't have the capacity." I told him he was right, and that it's still his responsibility. You don't need to know the preferences or primary appreciation language of your newest hire, but you need to know it for your direct reports. And you need your direct reports to know that you know it, not for free, but so that they know the preferences and primary appreciation languages of their direct reports, and so on. If my friend blindly sent flowers in appreciation to someone a skip-level or two down for behaving in a way that deserved recognition, that may be golden, but it *ain't* platinum. This, again, proves the value of having some sort of system—an intranet, for example—where people's appreciation language lives so you can easily look up what their reward and recognition preferences are to show up most effectively with and for them.

The Platinum Rule applies not just to rewards and recognition but also to feedback and assigning work. For example, as someone who appreciates making the implicit explicit, I've always had trouble being assigned work without explanation. Perhaps I'm not alone. A senior leader I used to work closely with knew that about me. So, whenever she sent along a new assignment, she'd accompany it with an email, text, phone call, or meeting request to provide further context. And she knew that would work well for me because she and I had both taken

Gretchen Rubin's Four Tendencies Quiz, which illuminates one's personality type (Upholder, Obliger, Questioner, or Rebel). My results showed I was a Rebel: I could be a brilliant performer under the right conditions—with an appropriate amount of urgency and information—but in their absence, I could end up resentful, digging my heels in and doing a less-than-stellar job, or procrastinating a task for a good, long while. That senior leader didn't do the same rigamarole for everyone on the team because it wasn't necessary for everyone else, though she knew it would go the extra mile for me and my motivation.

Insights like these keep you from "Golden Ruling" it. When you apply what you learn about others, you have the tools to follow the Platinum Rule, set the tone, and empower your team members to thrive on their own terms—for their betterment and that of the whole team and organization.

This is also why I believe leaders should have no more than five to ten reports, rather than twenty or more. It's up to you to understand each member of your team so you can amplify their strengths and mitigate their weaknesses. When you have more than a handful or two of reports, knowing them well enough to lead in a way that works best for them is hard. Few have the capacity for such an endeavor. And ultimately, it's up to you to treat people fairly but not uniformly.

I'm a big believer in the idea that a leader should have weekly meetings with their direct reports, and this important meeting is another reason to cap the number of direct reports. If you book a one-on-one with someone every two weeks and you miss a meeting, it could be a whole month before you connect with that direct report. That cannot be a setup for growth and success. So, I believe scheduling weekly meetings with your direct reports is the way to go.

These one-on-one conversations can be designed to:

1 **Check in**—to share what needs to be shared to be fully present in this conversation and one's week in general, which can include updates about things happening outside one's formal job, or work altogether, that may be affecting how they show up, for better or worse.

2 **Build deeper relationships**—with each other and with one another's context.

3 **Form agreements, not just accountabilities**—design together what will get done in the days and weeks ahead and what support is required to complete the tasks. I believe accountabilities are assigned and agreements are mutual. I would rather design and agree on a path ahead. It's far more empowering than assigning a task.

Much like a performance review is not the ideal time for new feedback from a leader or manager, these one-on-one meetings shouldn't be the first time a delay, snag, or issue is shared. If a leader and their direct report form an agreement that won't be met, the leader or employee ought to communicate the issue promptly so they can better team together for the reality at hand.

These one-on-one meetings are a way to facilitate the Platinum Rule in your culture. When you deliver this personalized treatment to others, you're teaching them to do the same for their reports and, if they aren't formal people leaders, their peers. That's the only way to scale culture—one team and leader at a time. *Psst, pass it on.*

Choose Who Surrounds You

Leadership isn't just about whom *you're* influencing, it's also about who influences *you*. You've likely heard the cliché that you are the average of the five people you spend the most time with. I've found that adage holds true, and there's anthropology to prove it, which we'll cover in the next chapter. I've seen senior leaders fundamentally shift their behavior based on the changing makeup of their team and the people they surround themselves with—rising and falling to the quality and values of their peers.

Take the case of Isaac, an executive and founder at a small firm. At first, Isaac and his teammate Liza were close. While Isaac hired Liza and she reported to him in the early start-up days, the team was so small that they were virtually peers. Isaac and Liza collaborated on numerous projects and became each other's confidants. In those early days, Isaac asked Liza to promise him something. "If I ever start acting like a jerk, please tell me," he pleaded, "regardless of our roles or what else is happening in our lives." Liza agreed, but she thought she'd never have to confront him on this. Isaac was a good guy. He had his weaknesses and limitations—as we all do—but he seemed so intent on addressing them and helping others do the same. Over time, though, things changed.

The team grew, and Isaac and Liza collaborated far less than in those early, scrappy days of the start-up. Many new people joined the organization, and more distance and silos were created between Isaac and Liza on the organizational chart and in their relationship. When new key players came on board—drivers with an opposite perspective to Liza's on how to grow the business and people—she noticed a shift in Isaac. He no longer seemed interested in her ideas. When the team got together, Isaac was quick to dismiss Liza in front of the group, and he frequently turned to the team's newer members instead. Eventually, the organization's culture changed, and the decisions made at the top trickled down.

Along the way, Liza thought about fulfilling Isaac's request from those early days, but she felt the relationship and psychological safety between them had nearly disappeared—along with the speak-up culture that had once existed in the organization at large. She didn't know what he'd say or do if she called him on his behavior, and she was afraid to find out.

Another part of the problem was that the new people Isaac had brought on were like him; there were more commonalities between them than he had with Liza. The differences between Liza and Isaac that had previously formed a complement shifted to misalignment and tension. Isaac seemed to prioritize others' thoughts over hers because they frequently aligned with his own views. This created an echo chamber, which is always detrimental to—if not deadly for—a speak-up culture.

Issues like this play out in organizations all over the world, every single day. Those we surround ourselves with can influence how we behave. So, it's vital to consider the people closest to us. Building a diverse team, composed of people from different backgrounds, experiences, and perspectives, is not only the morally right thing to do but also good for business.

As we think about how best to support the leaders we oversee and our own well-being, let's consider two of the most powerful human forces I know: hope and each other.

Hope is optimism. It's the grounded belief that tomorrow can be better and that we have the agency to make it so. It's the idea that we may, at present, be stuck in a dark tunnel, weaving our way around pitch-black bend after bend. And while we may not even see the light, we still know it's there, somewhere. We can and will work to find it and bring it to life.

A big part of what makes us strong as a species is each other—community, a group of people who agree to grow together. If you lose hope, please phone a friend, or better yet, go visit them. Help them, or even volunteer to help anyone. Seek out people and experiences that remind you the light is out there, perhaps just around the next corner, and worth pursuing.

For me, one of those friends is Matt Tod.

I'm very good at giving up on myself. I do it plenty of times a day. But when I commit to someone else, such as Matt, I can do what I say I'm going to do. I won't do it for me, but I'll do it for the other person. For example, I might say I'm going to wake up tomorrow morning and go for a run before my kids get up. I might even set my alarm. But if I'm accountable only to myself, it probably isn't going to happen. I can already see myself hitting the snooze button.

Meanwhile, Matt is a personal development junkie and great friend. He works on improving himself and supporting others more than anyone I know. And if I were to text him right now and ask him if he'd like to go for a run with me at 5:30 tomorrow morning, he'd likely be up for it or find some way to support me. Because we live about an hour-plus drive away from each other, I'd call him, and we'd go for our run over the phone. But here's the best part. I wouldn't be showing up for me. I'd be showing up for him. This—community and supporting one another—is the key element of what makes us so powerful as a species.

The relationships we cultivate—our friendships, familial relationships, and professional relationships with colleagues, mentors, and coaches—in and of themselves, are leadership development training. They give us courage and empower us to rise to the challenges in front of us. As individuals, we're limited. We're not designed to walk about this planet, or any other, on our own. We're designed to go together because together we are remarkable, and stronger. This is the reason we need to find ways to support our leaders and better support one another. Because, after all, it is together—in community—that we grow most, both as individuals and as teams.

7

Culture Matters

> "The consciousness of an organization will seldom, if ever, surpass the consciousness of its leaders."
>
> **FREDERIC LALOUX**

ALL RIGHT. Back to pickle theory.

What happens when you put a cucumber in pickle brine? (No, this is not a joke. This is repetition.) Ten times out of ten, that cucumber turns into a pickle.

If you've met me, you've probably heard me say this (and I mentioned this already in chapter 3). Why do I continue to harp on the fermentation process of *Cucumis sativus*?

Because I can't emphasize enough how important environment is. Put a person in a particular environment, system, or culture, and their surroundings will undoubtedly influence—for better or worse—how they feel, think, and behave. The question is, is the organization's pickle brine making delicious, crisp, wonderfully seasoned pickles, or is it inadvertently taking perfectly sound cucumbers and creating too soggy, salty, sweet, or sour pickles? Even better, the brine can transform a pretty average, or even lackluster, cucumber into a wonderful pickle. Of course, this analogy holds true with people in our cultures.

No Shortcuts, No Finish Lines

To understand how to shift and improve our culture, we must understand how change occurs. I see it happening across three gears interconnected with and affecting culture: mindset, actions, and systems. Any of the three gears can be the starting place for change, and you need all three working together for culture change to be meaningful and to last.

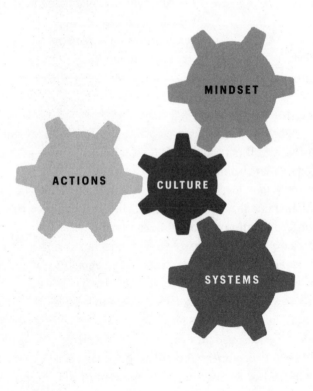

Mindset

When we shift our perspectives, we alter how we interact with others and the world around us and we get different results. As speaker and author Peter Docker taught me, a transformation is when nothing has changed yet everything is different, because we are different.

I am skeptical of senior leaders who seemingly turn on a dime and trade a profit-first mentality for one that puts their people and purpose at the center. Are they shifting their leadership from the inside out or the outside in? Are they leading a change because they have been genuinely inspired and transformed, or have public and external pressures made this shift in rhetoric opportune or a requirement? The latter is likely no change at all. It's more likely manipulation.

We may have seen this in an August 2019 announcement from the Business Roundtable (BRT), a non-profit lobbyist association based in Washington, DC, whose members are chief executive officers of major US companies. A declaration, signed by 181 CEOs, redefined the purpose of a corporation to promote "an economy that serves all Americans." That's very nice. I'm not against it. It would be even nicer and healthier to include nations and citizens beyond the United States because, after all, we are a global economy and can choose to be global citizens. But I won't harp on that too much. I have read the announcement and, while I appreciate the effort and sentiment, I wasn't inspired by its essence or by whom they selected as their spokespeople for this "groundbreaking" statement that conveniently caught up to public—customer, employee, and societal—opinion.

One of the BRT signers highlighted in the announcement was Jamie Dimon, CEO of JPMorgan Chase, who a few years before announced record-high layoffs in the exact same year that the company announced record-high executive bonuses. Gong! And marquee signer Alex Gorsky headed Johnson & Johnson, a company that was fined $572 million a mere week to the day following the BRT announcement for its involvement in the opioid crisis. Double gong! While the words read well, the say-do gap remains wide.

Real mindset transformation can look like this: Peter Docker, who is a few handfuls of years my senior, shared with me a distinct memory of going to the hospital with his then pregnant wife in labor. The delivery went well, and mom and baby were recovering and getting acquainted in hospital. The new parents agreed it would be wise for Peter to go back to their home and ensure everything was prepared for their impending return. As he re-entered the house, which he had left a mere day or two before, he noticed that the entire context had shifted. When he and his wife left the house, it was just that, their house. Upon his return, he appreciated that this was now the home where they would raise their children. Nothing had changed about their house, save for a bit more dust and ripened bananas, yet everything felt different. This is transformation. This is a true shift in mindset. When we shift our mindset, our actions shift, as do our results.

If more CEOs had an experience that made them realize that each of their employees is someone's precious child, and acted accordingly, as Bob Chapman teaches us, that BRT press release would mean more.

Among others, we should be studying leaders like Bob Chapman, CEO of Barry-Wehmiller; Indra Nooyi, former CEO of PepsiCo; and Hamdi Ulukaya, CEO of Chobani. In *Everybody Matters: The Extraordinary Power of Caring for Your People Like Family*, coauthor Chapman details how a good old American manufacturing company doesn't exist primarily to manufacture great machines or turn a healthy profit. It exists primarily to create extraordinary people who accomplish extraordinary things. These two quotes from Nooyi say it all:

"If you don't give people a chance to fail, you won't innovate. [And] if you want to be an innovative company, allow people to make mistakes." Upon reflecting on the future of the corporation she was heading, Nooyi writes, "I felt it was incumbent on me to connect what was good for our business with what was good for the world." Finally, Ulukaya, often called the "Anti-CEO," is using Chobani to make better food more accessible. He is an advocate of reducing income and wealth inequality nationwide and is doing so from the inside out of the company. Ulukaya implemented innovative profit-sharing and paid parental leave programs for Chobani's two thousand employees. The profit-sharing model gave 10 percent of the company to its employees. This isn't antithetical to profit and success. In less than five years, Chobani became the number-one-selling Greek yogurt brand in the United States, with more than a billion dollars in annual sales.

These three leaders, as examples, aren't putting their people and purpose first because it's popular or easy. They do it because it is right, and it is their belief. It is their true mindset, and, if you ask me, I don't believe they will sway.

Actions

Actions are where the rubber meets the road. Thomas Edison said, "Vision without execution is hallucination." If we start with a mindset shift and stop there, our head remains in the clouds while our feet float somewhere above the ground. We're not grounded or tactical enough to get anything done. Creating real change in ourselves, our people, and eventually our results requires us to act.

In his brilliant book *Turn the Ship Around!*, retired US Navy captain and bestselling author L. David Marquet refers to this concept as "acting your way to new thinking." In 1999, he took command of the worst-rated, worst-performing submarine in the entire US Navy fleet, the USS *Santa Fe*. Marquet wanted a quick win to boost morale on board. He wanted his sailors to feel proud to be a part of this crew and vessel. However, he couldn't force them to transform their mindset to be one of genuine pride. Pride isn't an order. So, instead, he crafted a simple and genius script that had the sailors act their way into the feeling.

Captain Marquet created a rule that whenever a guest was on board the *Santa Fe*, every crew member had to stop to greet them. They were ordered to look the guest in the eye, introduce themselves by their name, share what role they fulfilled on the submarine, shake the guest's hand, and say, "Welcome aboard the *Santa Fe*." Much like a mystery shopper, occasionally, one of these guests would be an evaluator.

On the crew's first evaluation while using this script, the evaluator, having never seen this behavior on any other vessel, noted that the sailors aboard the USS *Santa Fe* were proud to be a part of this crew and on this ship. Captain Marquet naturally shared the evaluation and positive review with his crew. The sailors contemplated it and thought they must be proud to be there. With this and an entire shift in how Marquet led— by giving control, not taking it—the *Santa Fe* went from worst to first, going on to achieve the highest retention and operational standings in the US Navy. Under Marquet's leadership, the *Santa Fe* also produced "a disproportionate number of officers and enlisted men to positions of increased responsibility, including ten subsequent submarine captains."

In the same way that the pride of the *Santa Fe*'s crew followed their actions, leaders can be effective in their roles before they genuinely care about their team members. I know. I'm shocked too. But allow me to explain.

Sometimes, people *want* to care, but they don't know *how* to care. Jen Marr, author of *Showing Up: A Comprehensive Guide to Comfort and Connection*, has spent years of her career in crisis response. She was part of the recovery team at the Sandy Hook Elementary School shooting, providing support for the school community every week for five years following the tragedy. She has experienced firsthand a world that is hurting and increasingly void of human connection, and she is determined to further the science and practice of human care and comfort. Marr teaches people how to extend their care, comfort, and connection to others. Not knowing what to say and do—not knowing how to care—can make things awkward. For example, in the case of Sandy Hook, people sent 67,000 teddy bears as gifts of comfort to a community with a population of twenty thousand. To feel cared for, people don't need a teddy bear or three. What they most need is human connection. They need to feel seen and heard, and that they and their experiences are valid and matter.

Marr has taught leaders to care for people, even if they don't know how or don't really want to, by equipping them with the types of questions to ask, such as, "How does that make you feel?" or "What matters about that for you?" She gives them actions to generate feelings of empathy, care, and comfort for others. Once we feel that human connection, we realize how powerful it is and may just want to feel it again. This is congruent with the work of psychologist Daryl Bem. He calls this "self-perception theory" and explains how we can act our way to change. Turns out, you can back into feelings, and into behavioral and culture change, by equipping people with some skills and actions to test out. Pretty cool.

Systems

Finally, systems matter—a lot. As I mentioned, when we place a seemingly good person in a bad system or environment, the latter almost always prevails. Systems and policies make it a real challenge for people to look beyond themselves, collaborate, and live their values. "That's the way it is," we say. "There's nothing I can do about it." Systems can directly or inadvertently lower our perceived impact and reduce the propensity for a speak-up culture.

One client I worked closely with for several years had a hard experience with this. It was truly a well-led company with bold and noble ambitions from the inside out. It manufactured and sold a product and service that could literally change people's lives and the course of history for the better. They make drones that keep people on the ground, like forest firefighters, out of harm's way. The company articulated a purpose that its leaders earnestly and tirelessly worked to bring to life, focused first on the internal culture: "to pioneer and innovate in all that we do, so that we radically improve the course of history." One such opportunity to bring their purpose to life came in offering promotions to deserving employees.

One employee was offered a promotion that would be life-changing for them. In accepting it, however, they would have to switch from one internal payroll system to another—a flaw in design. Because of this switch, this individual would have to go two weeks without pay, which they could not afford to do. The employee said they would love to accept the promotion and asked if they could circumvent the broken payroll system integration by receiving a pay advance to make the change possible for them. This request made it all the way up to the senior vice president of HR, who denied it. The CEO got wind of this and asked the HR leader what was going on. The HR leader said they didn't want to break policy. What were they thinking?

One lesson in this: we don't just trust people to follow the rules; we also trust them to know when it's a good time to break them. In the interest of "living your purpose for your people," this was one of those times for an exception to the rule.

To create real, lasting, and meaningful culture change in our organizations, we must pay attention to mindset, actions, and systems and know that they influence one another. Of course, we also must know and embody that, with culture, there is no arrival—we are constantly journeying. There is always more work to be done.

Dunbar's Number

As human beings, we aren't designed to form relationships at scale. We are a community-based animal. In our species' early days, we lived in groups of one hundred to 150 people. If we grew beyond that size, we would split off into two separate groups.

Ask someone today how many friends they have, and they may answer 5,143. No, no. Not social media followers—true friends. People whose names you know, whose lives you know meaningful details about. And you know how you're connected with them. We have a limited capacity for the number of relationships we can maintain because of the limits of time and our biological makeup. It's just who we are and how we're wired.

"Dunbar's number" refers to the work of British anthropologist Robin Dunbar, who identified the number of stable social relationships we humans can manage. If you were at a coffee shop and someone you knew walked in and you felt comfortable inviting them to join you for a conversation, that would likely be a stable social relationship. We aren't designed to care for thousands of people.

With some variance, human beings can maintain about 150 stable social relationships. Coincidence? I think not. For some of us the number is as high as 250 or as low as one hundred, though 150 is the average. Dunbar's research has shown that we spend 40 percent of our social time with the top five people in our social network and 20 percent of our social time with the next ten people in our network. That's 60 percent of our social time dedicated to fifteen people. This provides more context for why we should have five to ten direct reports, maximum, and gives proof to the claim that we are the average of the five people with whom we spend most of our time.

Let's relate this to our organizational cultures and how we can organically scale them. A CEO who says, "I care deeply about all twenty thousand of our employees" is lying. Biologically, they simply cannot. What they can do is say something like:

> There are twenty thousand people who show up to work every day at our organization. While I wish I could have a personal relationship with each and every one of you, I simply can't. I may not meet some of you for many years, and I regret to say that we may never meet face-to-face at all. What I do know with 100 percent certainty is that you have a leader, and you have a team. I see it as my job to care deeply for the people whose names I know, whose lives and careers I directly see and impact every day. I commit to supporting them, listening to them, and equipping them with what they need to thrive, here and beyond. I don't do that work for free, however. I do that work so that the people in my span of care extend it, in their own way, to the people in their span of care, and so on and so forth. Even though I may never meet all twenty thousand of you who work here, my commitment is to create the condition that you are cared for by your leader and the people around you.

That is how you scale culture.

An advantage and challenge of today is that we can cultivate meaningful relationships online. Such feelings are amplified and solidified by in-person meetings, but the Internet undoubtedly brings value. We can form communities—through our work, careers, and certainly beyond—using our values and beliefs as guides. Relationships built upon our values and beliefs are known as "psychographic relationships" and they often know no borders.

A leader's whisper is a shout,

and their tiptoes are stomps.

Within our society, organizations, or customer base, how might we help people find humanity in one another and establish a culture we're proud of?

It's best done and proliferated one leader, department, and team member at a time. And for the sake of progress, it is far more impactful to focus appropriate time and effort on those fifteen people with whom we spend 60 percent of our time. This is because we aren't so much loyal to organizations as we are to people. As the adage goes, "People don't quit organizations, they quit bosses." That's why cultures proliferate most powerfully on an interpersonal level.

When we think of organizations with seemingly great cultures, larger-than-life CEOs or senior leaders often spring to mind—people who have charismatic and dynamic personalities. I'm sure you've already thought of at least a couple. While the behavior of those and all leaders matters a lot, for culture to scale and remain healthy, the holders of the culture need to be everywhere, top to bottom and back up. Those in the middle— managers—a position I have been in for much of my career, hold a ton of influence.

The rhetoric is that we shouldn't behave as managers, we should behave as leaders. The term "manager" has acquired a negative connotation, and I've been guilty of feeding that flame in the past. But I've come to realize two things:

1. We need managers to create sustainable change.
2. And a lot of people hold that title.

Chances are we've been a manager, are in that role now, or know many people who have that title. Managers are the only people inside an organization who have multidirectional power—they can influence up, down, and side to side. I have seen organizations transform for the better when led from the middle. Although we need more managers who behave as leaders, we shouldn't bash the "manager" title. Culture and organizational success often live and die in the middle.

The Culture Equation

While the behavior of all team members matters, we are a hierarchical species. In our organizations, some people's values and behaviors undoubtedly matter a little more. Let's explore what it truly means to have a strong culture and how every individual in an organization can influence that culture, positively and otherwise.

We have values so we can live them. And whether we do or don't live them is the ultimate test of our culture. As business consultant and author Ken Blanchard once told me, and I'm paraphrasing here, if people repeatedly behave in a way that violates your organization's values after you've provided feedback and coaching, you can feel free to offer them to the competition. Let them wreak havoc over there.

Values are also an extremely important tool for decision-making. When the going gets tough and you need to make a hard decision and you don't know what to do, you can—and should—lean on those values as a litmus test. They'll inform you and your team how best to move forward in a way that authentically represents your organization and your own integrity.

$$\text{Culture} = (\text{Values} \times \text{Behavior})^{\text{Influence}}$$

The strength of a culture is determined by the clarity of the values multiplied by the behavior of its people. If you have clear values and don't live them, you get nothing—or worse. Your culture will surely be weak. Anything multiplied by zero is zero. Anything positive multiplied by a negative is a negative. If you don't have clearly defined values, or if you do but your people live counter to them (there's that say-do gap again), you will likely find yourself with a toxic, deleterious culture.

That's just part of the equation. The culture equation is also weighted by a person's influence. The more influence someone has in an organization, the more their values and behavior affect the culture. Influence can come in the form of seniority or authority, though not always. I have been in roles within an organization where I have next to no authority, but I've had influence because of my tenure, my role, and my relationships with senior leaders—the ones with the authority. While I didn't have the title, people still watched what they said to me or even buttered me up—because they knew I could influence the key decision makers. No title, no authority, but certainly influence. When one has influence, when one is a leader—whether by title or behavior—one's whisper becomes a shout and tiptoes become stomps.

Often, I find leaders and organizations articulate their values as nouns or adjectives. They're words that look good on walls, websites, or screensavers. In fact, the first time I found the company's values at my first job was months after I started, when I happened to keep my computer idle for fifteen minutes and the screensaver popped up. *Oh, Respect, Integrity, Communication, Excellence. Who knew?!* While those are nice words, they're kind of meaningless. Case in point: those four words were the values of Enron—an energy corporation whose accounting scandal, propagated by unethical leadership, caused its 2001 bankruptcy and demise.

Let's use Enron as an example, to see how we can transform values into something more actionable and meaningful:

- "Respect" could become "Treat people like the human beings they are."

- "Integrity" could be "Say and do the right thing, especially if it's hard and no one is looking."

- "Communication" could be "Listen first and communicate clearly, consistently, and often."

- "Excellence" might become "Do more of your great work."

"Integrity" is a hard one because it's subjective and the context matters. As Rich Diviney taught me, the definition of "integrity" for a Boy Scouts group is different from the definition of integrity for a terrorist group. Integrity as expressed and enacted in their behaviors and contexts will appear grossly different. This makes it ever important to define what you mean by integrity in your culture based on observable behaviors.

As for "communication": you aren't communicating enough until you get bored of your own message (repeated typically seven to eight times and in different formats—spoken, written, and recorded). As organizational psychologist Adam Grant highlights from a study on leadership communication, the data shows that leaders are nine times more likely to be criticized for under-communicating than overcommunicating. Those who say too little come across as unclear and uncaring. To tell if you're great at delivering a message, ask for feedback to see if your message lands. Have your listeners repeat what they heard but in their own words. See how broken or plugged-in the telephone is. Great communication has just as much, if not more, to do with great listening. The cliché that we have two ears and one mouth for a reason has great truth and power to it. Indeed, the most interesting people are the most interested people.

For me, "excellence" leads the list of meaningless values. "Would you do me a favor? Act with more excellence for the rest of the day, please." What the heck does that mean, and can you do anything about it? "Do more of your great work" gives us a way better chance of executing something meaningful, both individually and as a team. With that, we can amplify our strengths and mitigate or ask for help in our limitations.

Now, I'm not suggesting that in the case of Enron a simple shift in language would have reversed an entire scandal, propagated by their most senior leaders. At least as action phrases, their values would have been easier to execute, recognize, and reward in others. They could have been used as a basis for decision-making and providing feedback, coaching, or discipline to help close that say-do gap.

All leaders and organizations could adopt this lesson: our values are real and meaningful only if they are behaved, and it behooves us to let our people know what that behavior looks like.

What Comes First?

With an idea of how culture works, how to scale it, and how to bring it to life, you may be thinking about which population to prioritize when developing your culture. Across industries, there's a lot of talk about who comes first: employees or customers, educators or students, health practitioners or patients. My revelation, based on the culture equation, is none of the above.

Our *values* should come first because they dictate who our people are. Remember those psychographics.

A colleague of mine once saw a sticky note on a salesperson's computer that read, "If one of our customers asks you to do something that breaks one of our values, you're allowed to fire that customer." That's a great directive to work and live by.

In our household, my wife and I are crystal clear on the three values that guide the culture of our little organization, our family. We work hard to embody and instill these in our children. Our values are:

1   We treat people with kindness, care, and respect, regardless of whether we *like* them or not.

2 We are helper people; we can always help others (and find other helper people!).

3 We are allowed and encouraged to talk about our emotions, especially the hard ones.

Now, imagine that I invite a guest into our home for a meal—a potential client, let's say. I believe that if things go well, I'll land their business. That would be good! Impetus to put more food on the table for said family. But upon arrival, the guest disrespects my children and wife, behaving counter to one or more of our three foundational values and cultural pillars.

What I do next will indicate if our values are nice-to-haves and meaningless, or if they are indeed imperative.

If I don't have my family's back and I permit this guest to treat them poorly, I'm essentially saying to my family, "These are our values, only when it's convenient to me." Meanwhile, if I go so far as to inform this potential client of our family values—which they likely had no idea about when they walked into our home—I can ask them to act accordingly, or I'll ask them to leave. That would be integrity in action for the culture of our family. As legendary advertising creative director Bill Bernbach said, "A value isn't a value unless it costs you something."

Even though it's not a comfortable situation, I do have a choice: I can hold my tongue, protect the opportunity at hand, and put profit over the emotional well-being of my family. Or I can stand up for the people I claim are the most important people in my life. If I choose the latter, I'm communicating to my family that the values we espouse mean everything and they are guiding our actions forward. What a great example to set for my subordinates (my kids) and my partner. And if the client is the right fit, they will respect my decision and behavior. If they're the wrong fit, that will likely be that and we'll be left with more leftovers from that meal.

That is the goal—to use our values to guide our behavior. Our behavior will then attract the right people (employees, customers, and vendors alike) and repel those who aren't a fit anyway. This approach establishes the psychologically safe environment necessary for a speak-up culture. It lets people know that we're all in this together and on the same page. And that means when tough stuff comes up, we can address it together authentically, transparently, and consistently as a trusting and united team.

Make a Big Deal of the Little Things

I remember a lecturer of entrepreneurship from business school teaching me to make a big deal of the little things before the little things become a big deal. He was describing an experience in his career when he was responsible for launching a two-hundred-person start-up that was being funded and implanted within a forty-thousand-person company. Unlike the typical start-up growth process, where you have two people, then five, then fifteen, and the opportunity to develop culture alongside your burgeoning team, he was already above Dunbar's number of 150 on day one. All the people there—the vast majority of whom he hadn't met before he took the reins—brought their own assumptions about culture from their previous roles and experiences. Thus, he felt it was on him to establish culture ASAP. He described a few examples of going out of his way early on in that company, even when vulnerable and uncomfortable, to make a big deal out of the little things to overtly communicate and embody the values to establish the culture.

Liane Davey coins the avoidance of hard conversations as "conflict debt." The more we put off the little stuff, the more that debt builds, and we suddenly find ourselves in an ineffective and resentful relationship.

In my own company, when I hired employee number one, Alejandro, I went out of my way to provide feedback on the littlest things. We still do so today. Many times, I debated in my head whether something was worth bringing up, but I usually did voice it. If I had feedback that could make his work, our relationship, and our little company better, why would I sit on it? I was mindful about practicing the Platinum Rule and trying to deliver the feedback when and in ways it would be best heard. Per his request, I often wrote out the feedback first and sent it to him ahead of discussing it—that helped him process it (English is his second language) and come to our discussion with a grounded perspective. I worked hard to deliver the feedback respectfully and with a belief that I may not be right. It was this repeated practice of making a big deal of the little things, especially toward the beginning of our relationship, that helped us avoid big and bad things from transpiring. We quickly became good at having the difficult conversations that would help each other grow, keep our conflict debt low, and give us good practice for when bigger and harder decisions and conversations transpired. It was never easy, but it got easier, and it's always been worthwhile.

A Dynamic Perception

A speak-up culture—where it's safe and worth it to share our ideas, concerns, disagreements, and mistakes—is not just a seal we can stamp on our organization's website, walls, service vehicles, or anywhere else and then forget about. That label must be earned by the organization and its leaders every single day. A speak-up culture is a deeply personal experience with those who have influence on our careers—whether they be our peers, subordinates, or, especially, those in roles more senior than our own. Labeling our culture a speak-up culture or our organization one of the best places to work can be quite demotivating if that's not how our team members experience it. Imagine being in a meeting room where one of the walls says "Best Place to Work" and having to navigate a conversation with a boss whom you feel is bullying you. That kind of thing happens every day around the globe.

The greatest leaders and organizations prioritize bringing these labels to life from the inside out. The truth is, just as you must earn the designation of being called a "leader" from those you serve, or a "great teammate" from those you work with, those organizational culture badges must also be earned, repeatedly and in perpetuity. I know, it's hard. But it's the cost of real leadership.

Everyone's truth is their own perception. That means when someone reports an experience that's different from your own, it's your responsibility and opportunity to understand the full picture—to get and stay curious. This could be about a project that may going off the rails, a leader who is potentially behaving poorly, or an idea to improve the operation. And even if only one person is seemingly experiencing this, you must take their idea or concern seriously, while treating all parties fairly, with dignity and respect.

Along the way, you may uncover a values mismatch, or possibly mental health concerns that require a different approach. You'll remember that, as Liane Davey explains, a person may fear an aversive outcome or hold their own baggage—all of which contributes to the way they perceive their world. It serves us to determine which of these issues, or what potential mix of factors, are relevant in a particular situation. We can surely ask for help to sort it out and decide how best to proceed.

You may not be able to make everyone feel psychologically safe all the time. After all, psychological safety and impact are perceptions. Though you can always do what is in your control—show concern and care, listen, and try to improve constantly. You also will not retain every employee who joins your team for all time. Relationships and organizations evolve. That's normal and can even be healthy.

I've heard leaders tell employees that the team isn't their therapist when the employees voiced concerns about managing the demands of work and life, and I've heard leaders say that any issues employees have are their own problems. I've witnessed leaders take feedback from subordinates as an indictment rather than as insight into real struggles unfolding at various levels of an organization. When someone builds the courage to bring something they've been experiencing to our attention, it's up to us to address it properly. To listen, to believe their experience is valid, and to show them we care. That may mean resisting the urge to shove it under the rug, dismiss them, or keep marching on. It means striving to meet your people's needs and helping them get the support to thrive. Ultimately, don't we want people to enjoy their work, feel engaged and fulfilled, and give it their all for the team?

Everyone is right when it comes to their experience and emotions. And we can always find ways to support people and do our best to help them thrive, even if they end up doing so on another team or at a different organization.

Remember, too, that people are watching. If you truly want a healthy, thriving speak-up culture, you must encourage people to use their voice, and when they do, reward them for it, if indeed you wish for their truth to keep coming. This isn't a hall pass for people to share whatever they want, to whomever they want, in whatever way they want to. Respect, dignity, tact, and an intention of improvement can still be table stakes for a speak-up culture. But if you truly wish to hear the ideas, concerns, disagreements, and mistakes from people so that you can constantly improve as leaders and as an organization, then encouraging and rewarding people for speaking up are the key.

8

The Virtuous Cycle of "Encourage and Reward"

"I'd rather get bad news from an honest man than lies from a flatterer."

URSULA K. LE GUIN

"**THANK YOU** for telling me. You're fired."

These were words shared by a student in a class taught by Scott Sonenshein, author and professor of management at Rice University. While the class was discussing the importance of psychological safety, the student told a story about a former colleague of hers when she worked on an offshore oil rig. The colleague had mistakenly and unknowingly damaged some drilling equipment while on the job—not good.

The vessel's captain addressed the entire crew, requesting that the person who was responsible for the damage come forward so that they could all learn from it and move on. Shortly afterward, the colleague did step forward and take responsibility.

They explained exactly what happened and said they were unaware of the damage until the captain made the crew aware of it. And in response, the captain said, "Thank you for telling me. You're fired."

What an ideal way to obliterate a speak-up culture. The worst part of this example is the gaping say-do gap. Had the captain instead said, "We need to find out who is responsible for this damage so that we can take appropriate corrective action," that would be a different story. But because the captain said, "We need to learn from the mistake," they made the crew, and particularly the crew member who made the mistake, feel that it was safe and worth it to speak up. Evidently, it was not.

We can all guess what will happen the next time someone makes a mistake on the rig. No one will own up to it. People will spend more time and energy hiding mistakes, sweeping them under the rug rather than owning up to them and trying to improve. Would you blame them?

The crew on this oil rig have now been conditioned to believe that if they admit they went wrong somewhere, they may be fired. And as we know from Amy Edmondson's hospital study mentioned earlier, just because there are fewer errors reported doesn't mean there are fewer errors occurring. With a lack of psychological safety, the opposite is more likely to be true, and to compensate, people spend an inordinate amount of time hiding their mistakes.

True leaders foster a culture that encourages people to speak up and rewards them when they do, especially in sharing the tough stuff. The second and equally fundamental part of the cycle, reward, is often forgotten. A reward need not be in the form of a raise, bonus, promotion, or statue made in one's honor. It is about ensuring that whoever spoke up is acknowledged and feels that their contribution was truly heard, valued, taken into consideration, and even acted upon. This way, the perceived risk of speaking up is lower, the impact is higher, and they and others around them will be more likely to speak up again.

That creates a cycle in which people speak up when they have something to say, regardless of how difficult it may be, because they believe it is safe, that they won't be ignored or punished for doing so, and that it will create some positive change in the organization, for its people, results, and culture.

Ripples In All Directions

There was a time when I was very much in the middle of middle management at an organization. While I didn't have much authority, I did have influence. I had the ear of the people who had the authority. During that time, I, and others at my level and below, felt that an earnest, hardworking member of our team was being treated and evaluated unfairly. It appeared to me that the senior leadership team was not seeing the full picture about this person and that there could be a better perspective for all to take. But I was hesitant to speak up. I wasn't sure how the organization's leaders would respond.

A colleague of mine, Irene, had a similar read on the situation. We both worked closely with the struggling team member, so Irene and I discussed what we could do. Together, we decided to draft an email to the senior leadership team stating that we wanted to talk through the situation. Irene hit "send," cc'ing me and cosigning the email. *Gulp.*

When the leadership team agreed to meet with us and invited us to attend a portion of their next weekly meeting, we were encouraged to share our point of view. And ultimately, we were rewarded for it. That didn't mean we received more money, a promotion, or that they followed every bit of our advice. The reward was far more intrinsic. One of the most senior leaders at the meeting expressed how grateful she felt that people in the organization outside the leadership team cared so much about the culture, the team, the individuals on it, and the values we had all agreed to uphold. Everyone thanked us for having the guts to step up and speak up. It felt good. It felt right. I felt rewarded.

We weren't sure what change would come of it, but we left feeling that we'd done what we could—that the risk to speak up, in that moment, felt worth it. Even though we weren't in charge, we shared our thoughts and aimed to use what influence we did have for the better. It felt risky, and it was hard—I could feel the fear and my heartbeat in my ears as we parted the ropes and the spotlights beat down on us as we entered into the "speak-up boxing ring," if you will—but because the senior leadership team heard us out and made us feel that they were grateful for our insight, courage, and help, we were willing and able to do it again. In fact, I spoke up more in subsequent interactions with senior leaders on that team because of that experience. I continued to feel that I was improving the culture, strategic decisions, and results of the organization by doing so. Using my voice felt truly encouraged and rewarded. I felt I mattered.

But what's more, when asked about the meeting by our peers, we reported back that the conversation went well, and we encouraged them to consider broaching tough topics with leadership as well. And so, one positive interaction rippled through the organization for the better, creating the potential for more speak-up conversations ahead.

Contrast this with an experience of one of my clients, Sam, who had been an instrumental part of a growing technology company. He held several key positions and received multiple promotions during his near fifteen-year tenure. Sam had been a valued member of the team, for his work, voice, and contribution to the company's results and culture.

A change in the leadership team members prompted what Sam, and apparently many others, felt was a significant shift in the behaviors of its leaders. Sam thought their behaviors and decisions were increasingly short-sighted and driver-like. He was concerned the organization and its leaders were losing their way.

Up until this point, Sam had helped lead the culture of the company in partnership with the CEO and founder, Ross; in fact, Ross had described Sam as a spiritual leader of the team's culture. One day at a weekly leadership team meeting that Sam was invited to attend, Ross prompted Sam to share a pulse read of the team's morale. While this was in Sam's wheelhouse and a fair question, it threw him off. The question was blunt and unexpected, and he didn't quite feel safe enough to answer honestly in front of some of the leaders, whom Sam felt were a significant source of the problem. He answered Ross's question cautiously and diplomatically. And although he shared truthfully, Sam did not share his entire truth. That conversation fizzled and the meeting moved on to its regular agenda.

But after the meeting, Sam felt distraught and conflicted. He knew he had more to say but feared how it would be received. He sought sound counsel and coaching and then decided: he couldn't go to sleep in good conscience that night without confronting what he believed was truly going on. Sam called Ross that evening.

"What's up?" Ross said.

"I wasn't completely forthright with you today when you asked me about the team's morale," Sam said. "I think we have some morale and cultural issues at the company."

Sam felt as though Ross were rolling his eyes on the other end of the phone. "I've heard this complaint before," Ross said. "Please, give me some specific examples so that I can do something about it."

Indeed, this CEO had heard such complaints from other employees in recent years and a clear pattern was visible in the company's culture. But every other person who had previously uttered similar feedback was no longer at the company—they were made to be the problem and they either resigned or were fired.

Sam pressed on. He had already ripped off the bandage and it felt too important to remain silent. He shared nearly everything he had experienced, felt, and seen in others, respecting his team members' privacy along the way. Sam cited examples of when he felt and saw that certain leaders were behaving outside the proclaimed value set and behaviors of the company and leadership team—senior leaders yelling at and demeaning more junior employees, leaders putting deadlines and results ahead of people's well-being, leaders pointing fingers at others and taking next to no responsibility themselves, and so on. It wasn't easy sharing this feedback, but it felt like the right thing to do.

As the call was ending, Ross thanked Sam for speaking up and said, "Leave it with me."

Sam thought for a moment and then pushed back, "I don't want to leave it with you. We're supposed to own the culture together. I want to be a part of the solution."

Ross sounded distant when he said, "Okay," and then hung up the phone. Sam still remembers the length of the call, seeing 36:42 on his phone as he hung up.

Despite the snag at the end, Sam still felt a sense of catharsis after the conversation. Months of fear, anxiety, and pressure eased. He slept well that night for the first time in a long time.

But the feeling was short-lived.

The next day was a great one for Sam, if busy. He felt energized by the conversation with Ross the previous evening. Late that afternoon, he saw that he had missed a call and then a text message from Ross asking him to call back. Sam assumed Ross was circling back to expand on the conversation, provide an update, and continue to address the issues together as cultural co-leaders.

When Sam got a chance to call Ross toward the end of the business day, Ross picked up quickly.

"Your claim that we have a team morale issue is a serious indictment," were Ross's first words. "There is no team morale issue. The morale issue is with you."

It felt like a punch in the gut. Sam couldn't believe it. He was shocked. He even laughed a little, in disbelief, at how Ross's perspective seemed to have shifted 180 degrees on the matter in less than twenty-four hours.

This conversation was much shorter than the one the previous evening. It also wasn't really a conversation. Ross had a message to deliver. Sam confirmed with him: "So I'm guessing I can't bring this issue back to you again?"

"Yup. That's right," Ross said. After a pause, he continued, "Though you can always come to me for coaching." In other words, Sam could go back to Ross for help, so long as he showed up knowing that he himself was the problem. This seemed like classic gaslighting.

Sam felt attacked and wronged, and that it was certainly no longer safe and worth it to speak up. Within a couple of months, Sam was quietly demoted from the leadership team. He became dejected, reserved, lacking in confidence, and so unlike how he

Focus on encouraging your people to share their truth, and on rewarding it, especially if it's bad or hard news to hear.

had been at his best. It's as if the pickle brine of the company had starkly changed. Sam confided in a few close teammates, and the team around him saw how he felt and behaved through this time. Those ripples negatively impacted others on the team and their decision to speak up. It was more likely they'd keep quiet. Eventually, Sam left the company, feeling like an old gazelle who had been pushed out to the fringes of the pack—unsupported, unprotected easy pickings.

Sam did bounce back and became better off because of this situation, but it was not a fun, healthy, or productive number of months.

The real shame is what the organization lost when Sam left: a loyal and devoted team member who was willing to speak up, take a risk, and share what he genuinely felt would improve the organization, its people, and its results.

Encourage (How to Feed a Deer)

What's the distinction between encouraging and rewarding? How do you know when one stops and the other begins?

I like to think of encouragement like feeding a deer. You put your hand out but don't make eye contact (if you do, the deer will likely get scared and run away), and hope for a majestic experience that your friend will record on video for the 'gram. Just as you cannot force a deer to take acorns from your palm, you cannot force someone to speak up. All you can do is focus on the conditions you are creating as a leader—the mindset, actions, and systems you amplify—to build trusting relationships with the people in your span of care. Trust begets vulnerability. It's trust—psychological safety and perceived impact—that will help make it safe and worth it for people to speak up.

Encouragement is imperative. A belief or willingness to value what others share is certainly helpful. As Amy Edmondson explains, "The basic human challenge is this: it's very hard to learn when you already know. If I could keep reminding myself that I don't know, then I open myself up to learning. If you want people to commit, heart and soul, to working in your organization, you better be listening to them."

When people believe you want to hear from them, they're more likely to step up and use their voice. When you encourage others, you open the channels of communication and make way for their insights—their ideas, concerns, disagreements, and mistakes—to flow in.

An active approach to encouragement may be sharing with your team, "It's vital that I hear your perspective." You can also tell on yourself, saying something like, "I'm not getting any feedback, but here's what I think my feedback may be. Am I on point or off base here?" Then the key is to zip it, use silence, ask another open-ended question if needed, and reward whatever feedback comes your way. Reward what you feel is the truth, not just a sugar-coated version of it. Being vulnerable, humble, and speaking up first may be the impetus your people need to believe you want to hear from them, especially if it's bad news. No one likes calling the boss's idea bad. The greatest leaders welcome that kind of feedback and create the conditions for it.

There are very few people who we can all agree are or were good leaders. One, I would argue, is Nelson Mandela. I'd like to hear the debate that says Mandela was an ineffective leader. A perfect human? Doesn't exist. An effective leader? I think so.

In his own leadership, Mandela was undoubtedly and deeply influenced by his father, who was a tribal chief and community leader. As a young boy, Mandela would often accompany his father to community meetings, and he would consistently observe two things:

1 His father, in his role as chief, would insist people sit in a circle. There is no apex in a circle, so although there can

still be some hierarchical dynamics, the circle denotes equality and sets the tone for speaking up. Everyone in the circle
can make eye contact with one another.

2 His father would speak last. By the time it was his turn to
speak, he had gained from the ideas, perspectives, thoughts,
and questions from the entire group. The group made him
smarter, not the other way around.

I have attended countless meetings where the most senior
leader in the room kicks it off by saying, "Okay, everyone. We
have this issue. We need to solve it. I need your best ideas and
thinking. Here's what I think..." Do not do this! Speaking last
and suspending your opinion, especially as the most senior person in the room, gives others the space to share their thoughts,
ideas, and questions. Otherwise, you're more likely to cause
groupthink, or stifle the team's ideas and opinions: "Sure thing,
boss. Your idea sounds great." Create the environment in which
others can speak up first, and ensure that you're not always
hearing from the same voices. Encourage ideas and especially
dissenting points of view from the most diverse group possible.
This is how you gain from the true collective genius. And, of
course, once people do share—especially the hardest things to
share and especially when the least heard or most marginalized
people speak up—you must reward them, or their voices will
disappear.

In an interview, Edmondson describes a talk she had with a
pilot named Ben Berman, who is an expert in aviation safety. He
described his flight routine to her, complete with active encouragement. Every single time he flew, he met with his entire crew
and shared, "I've never flown a perfect flight and today is no
exception." Edmondson says, "That seems a strange way for a
very expert, very thoughtful, educated person to start the flight.
But he's saying, 'You have an invitation to speak up. I need you.'"

He's actively encouraging the team to tell him what they see. Cue the well-known safety tagline: when you see something, say something.

Another way to encourage people to speak up is to strip titles to create greater humanity and equity, much as Mandela's father attempted to do by sitting in a circle at meetings. I've heard of a cardiac surgeon at a world-famous hospital who insists everyone goes by first names in the operating room. This flattens the hierarchy and lowers the bar to speak up.

If gathering qualitative feedback proves to be challenging, organizational psychologist Adam Grant suggests making things quantitative, with a question like, "On a scale of zero to ten, how good do you feel about our approach to this challenge?" And if all you're getting back is tens, consider the possibility that people are not comfortable speaking up or sharing their true thoughts and feelings. Ask them for their votes and then ask them what made them select that number. If it's easier and safer to start with anonymity, go for it.

For more insight, invite them to add a few words to justify the answers they've given. For example, you might say, "Team, I'm working on my ability to get my ideas across simply, effectively, and succinctly. I really want to know how I'm doing. On a scale of zero to ten, how clear and succinct was that presentation? You don't need to share your name. Keep it anonymous if you prefer. Please consider providing your rating and kindly expand on it with a few words to help me understand. Thank you."

Passive routes of encouragement can be just as important, especially since they offer means of gathering feedback anonymously. A 2021 *State of Employee Feedback* report from AllVoices, an employee relations management platform, found that 74 percent of employees would be more apt to share their feedback if they knew they could do so anonymously. A more passive take may include an anonymous suggestion box—

.either physical or digital—or third-party hotline that encourages people to provide their feedback or even report issues. Ultimately, a sign of a thriving speak-up culture may be one in which it is safe and worth it to put your name next to your feedback or share it face-to-face. But if given the choice of gaining no input or gaining from anonymous input, I'd prefer the latter.

Surveys can provide important insight too. Regardless of how you gather that feedback, you must act on it. The same report found that 40 percent of employees need to see something done about what they've shared to feel as if they were heard. This seems intuitive. Why speak up repeatedly or respond to surveys if it won't lead to any improvements? Meanwhile, 41 percent of employees left a job because they didn't feel heard, and 37 percent moved on because they felt their feedback wasn't taken seriously.

Reward (A Genuine Thank-You May Do)

Rewards for speaking up need not be extrinsic, such as a raise, bonus, or promotion. A reward for speaking up can often be intrinsic, something as simple as "thank you," or "That must have been hard to share. Please keep it coming." It could be, "Well, that sucks to hear, but I think you're right. I'm thankful you brought this up. We need to dig in, learn more, and do something about this." Or even, "We didn't implement your idea. Here's why. Please keep the ideas and questions coming. They're great and they're what we need to keep getting better."

One thing I teach people to do to become more effective communicators is to complete conversations. How often do we start a conversation and not end it, whether that's in a one-on-one or group setting? I call these finished, rather than complete, conversations. You end them abruptly because of a time pressure—the next meeting, task, commitment, or picking up your kids from soccer practice. Great communicators close the loop. "Hey, I've got to run, *and* this conversation is finished but not complete. Let's complete it. How's Thursday afternoon?" Closing the loop is a form of reward and your effectiveness as a leader and communicator is likely to skyrocket.

By now, you've heard me say that we get the behavior we reward, and we get the behavior we tolerate. Toleration is a form of reward too. It's indirect and passive, but it reinforces behavior. Toleration may be putting up with toxic behavior from a great individual performer or avoiding giving feedback to a difficult team member—both scenarios reward those individuals and punish the rest of the team.

Keep people's Languages of Appreciation in mind as you're considering a reward and recognition (or feedback, for that matter... more on that in the next chapter). Would they prefer to be acknowledged one-on-one, or in front of others? Would it be more meaningful to send a handwritten note, flowers, a gift card, or a meal (homemade or otherwise)? Meaningful rewards ensure your team members feel seen, valued, and appreciated. And you'll be more likely to see the same behavior you're rewarding repeated.

I have seen this through performance management as well. Some high-trust and high-performance team members aren't given extrinsic rewards, not because they aren't deserving but because of market conditions, organizational performance, or charting employees' performance on a bell curve. Oh, bell curves. Good for when you should have failed that statistics exam. Not as good when it diminishes your performance rating from "exceeds" to "meets expectations." In other words, when conditions beyond your control make extrinsic rewards untouchable, intrinsic rewards can still be of great value and motivation. Use the Platinum Rule. Find out and focus on a person's career goals and support them. What do they enjoy doing or need most outside of work? Support them or provide it. While we ought to compensate people fairly, feeling rewarded, valued, and that you matter goes well beyond dollars and cents.

What About Bad News?

Recognizing and acknowledging that a problem or difficulty exists ought to be rewarded as well, especially if something is shared with an aim to create improvements. As the saying goes, "Bad news never gets better with time."

I had the opportunity to deliver a keynote on leadership and culture to the managers of an organization that does important work to keep people safe on a national level. The organization employed about twenty thousand people at the time, fifteen hundred of whom were managers.

During the pre-engagement call, I spoke with the event's executive sponsor. I liked him immediately. He was passionate about the topic, and we listened to many of the same podcasts, read many of the same books, and seemed to share quite a few viewpoints on how leaders ought to behave and organizations ought to be led. I walked away from that videoconference meeting feeling like he was a good, earnest leader, which I don't feel about every leader I speak with on pre-engagement calls.

The day of the keynote arrived, and the executive sponsor was set to give remarks before me. When I can, I show up to events early, even virtual ones, and take in the remarks of other speakers. The context I often get, especially from internal presenters and executives, is gold . . . maybe even platinum! When I logged on, the address from that same executive sponsor I met on the pre-engagement call was underway. After his planned remarks, he opened the virtual floor for a live Q&A session with the managers. The second question was asked anonymously: "What is being done to combat managers' overwhelming workload and burnout?"

"Well," he responded, "we completed an initiative to address that four months ago, and I'm pleased with the results. I don't see an issue. Next question."

Dismissed. Yikes.

I was shocked and disappointed. I had thought this was a great leader—and I do believe he had the best of intentions—but the mere fact that the question was asked, despite the intervention that happened months before, meant that an issue with workload and burnout persisted. The executive had, perhaps, been put on the spot, but imagine the difference if he had said something like this:

> Thank you for the question. I know this has been a struggle, and I appreciate the courage to bring this up again. Here are the initiatives we have already completed and the results we have seen . . . I am proud of these results and what these programs have accomplished. But the mere fact that this question was still asked means there's more work for us to do.
>
> I'll admit that this is a surprise to me, but that doesn't mean what you are saying is untrue. Thank you for speaking up. We must and will investigate this and do more because our jobs are important and your ability to show up and perform matters for your work, families, and public safety. My hope and commitment to you is that by next quarter's all-hands meeting, this question need not be asked, and I will work, and rely on all your support, to make it so. Thank you.

That response, in and of itself, would have been a reward—acknowledging that the problem, which at least one and likely other people were experiencing, was valid and would be meaningfully addressed.

Dismissing and denying the issue was not an effective strategy by this senior leader. Can you imagine how those struggling or seeing their colleagues struggling with workload and burnout felt after that Q&A? The executive sponsor's response was, unfortunately and likely unintentionally, quite dejecting. It may even have caused a portion of employees to look for other jobs, quit quietly, or quit entirely. Which brings to light a harsh reality: As soon as you repeatedly ignore or, worse, punish people for speaking up, it no longer becomes worth the risk or the breath. You are more likely to get a culture of silence as a result. A "zip it" or "shut it" culture, not a speak-up culture.

So, if you want to cultivate a speak-up culture, focus on encouraging your people to share their truth and on rewarding it when it arrives, even if and especially if it's bad or hard news to hear.

9

Feedback Is a Dish Best Shared

"The single biggest problem in communication is the illusion that it has taken place."

GEORGE BERNARD SHAW

WAS PETRIFIED. I was sitting at a colleague's desk in her office. She, the founder and CEO, was in the meeting room down the hall saying her goodbyes to the clients for whom she had just led a full day's training on leadership, culture, and trust. The clients evidently loved her and her work, and for good reason: she was personable, authentic, dynamic, flexible, and darn good at her craft. As a speaker, facilitator, and leader, she was, and remains, the real deal.

I had been sent out to observe, provide feedback, and, hopefully, certify her to lead certain keynotes and workshops. And she failed.

A wise and very proper sixth-grade teacher of mine gave my parents this feedback during a parent-teacher interview:

"Stephen needs to rely upon more than his charm to get by."
Whoa. And she was right. To this day I can still be guilty of relying on my quick wit to get by rather than doing the hard work to prepare and rock it. *Shhh. Don't tell anyone.*

Now, sitting at my colleague's desk, waiting for her so we could debrief the session, I was preparing myself to deliver that very same feedback. It was an agonizing wait.

I remember staring at a great quote from Simon Sinek that she had printed out and taped to the bottom of her computer screen: "A boss who micromanages is like a coach who wants to get in the game. Leaders guide and support... then sit back and cheer from the sidelines."

As I went back and forth in my head about what to say, what not to say, and whether I should even speak up at all, this quote gave me the courage and, frankly, sense of responsibility to proceed. After all, this was a moment to practice the very work that my colleague and I espoused. The encouragement and safety in our relationship was present.

When she finally entered, we exchanged some awkward pleasantries. I half stood up, inviting her to sit in her own chair. She insisted I stay where I was, as if reinforcing the power dynamic between us in that conversation.

My strategy was to get her talking first. "So, how do you feel it went?"

She took it easy on herself. "I felt it went okay..." she said.

Although we liked each other, we hadn't known each other for long. But we had enough trust and safety between us to be real with each other. And I had a job to do. I wasn't going to certify her, and I owed it to her to provide an explanation and honest feedback. I informed her that from my point of view, it hadn't gone well at all. She had pulled it off because she had enough raw talent, relationship with the client, and experience to do so. But it seemed to me she hadn't prepared nearly enough based on the material I was there to certify her on, and that she had been improvising her way through it. I had taken time out of my schedule, away from my wife, who was six months pregnant, to come and certify her, and I couldn't. Frankly, I felt as if my time had been wasted.

This conversation was hard, but my comments were received so well and with such humility. She didn't defend, deny, or try to explain herself. She even apologized. After that, the discussion was amazingly productive, and we ended up finding the best and right path ahead for all.

That was January 2016. All these years later, she continues to remind me of that moment, the difference it made in her life and career, and how it formed the basis of our now thriving friendship. Indeed, we've become each other's confidant, mentor, and coach: challenging, pushing, and supporting one another along.

This is a speak-up culture gone right. This was one of the most difficult yet rewarding conversations of my career to date. Because of our relationship and the context of it, I was encouraged to speak up. And, when I did, it was surely rewarded. It's made subsequent opportunities to speak up with her safe, easier, and worth entering.

The Case for Candor

Crucial to a speak-up culture is the ability to have healthy and productive feedback conversations. Feedback isn't fact, it's opinion. The purpose of feedback is to initiate meaningful dialogue that builds deeper connections and better relationships—to help one another grow. Feedback is not a dish best *served*, it is a dish best *shared*.

Earlier, I mentioned "candor with care," a concept I've adopted from Kim Scott's brilliant book *Radical Candor*. Radical Candor, as Scott says, entails caring personally and challenging directly.

Challenging directly without caring personally is what Scott calls "Obnoxious Aggression." In many cultures, it is far easier to care personally than to challenge directly. Scott calls this "Ruinous Empathy," which is all about "being nice." It may be *nice* to avoid giving hard, truthful, and clear feedback, but it isn't kind, and it doesn't help us grow. We often rationalize the withholding of feedback because, we claim, we don't want to hurt someone's feelings or put a major dent in their self-confidence. In truth, we are often protecting ourselves by shying away. We are afraid. But the best bosses are not the ones who let people coast. The best bosses help people grow. Candor with care, and not Ruinous Empathy, contributes to that growth.

Being forthright is daunting. But if we don't challenge someone directly when it's called for, it can be a disservice to ourselves and, especially, to others. Caring is key here, however. Challenging someone without care for them can be aggressive and diminishing. Being actively kind means exhibiting the courage and grace to share with honesty and to show up to help a person improve.

A telltale sign of true psychological safety is the ability to disagree and do it well; to debate with tact, respect, and authenticity; and to dissect ideas, not people. The discomfort or tension in these conversations is viewed as a necessary vehicle for progress.

Notice Your Rank

As a leader, you are in a position of authority. You have influence and your words and actions bear more weight than others with less seniority or influence (remember the influence component of the culture equation in chapter 7). Your position and authority affect how your feedback will be received. Again, your feedback is not fact; it's an opinion. To walk around the world believing otherwise is naive at best and narcissistic at worst. As leaders, it serves us to possess some humility in knowing that when we share our feedback with another, we are only sharing our experience. It's not the truth; it's only our version of the truth. That's why feedback is a dish best *shared*, not served.

Even the best cooks must taste their own food to make sure it's on point. If you dish out your feedback without soliciting and receiving any in return, you may eventually find that your dish (your behavior) stinks—but you haven't been tasting it. All great leaders look in the mirror, and invite feedback from others to help them do so.

One of the greatest ways to make feedback more effective in your teams and organization is by deliberately designing opportunities for it. So many people dread receiving feedback because the only time that "F-word" is uttered is when they've done something wrong and it's time for them to be chewed out, knocked down, reprimanded, or even humiliated. If you provide feedback only to criticize, do not be surprised if whoever is receiving it hears the score from the *Jaws* movie (*dun dun, dun dun, dun dun*) in the background any time you drop a note or pop by to let them know you have some *feedback* for them.

So, want to make sure your dish "don't stank"? Start with regular and frequent communication.

Call with Good News, Call Often

As an interior decorator, my mom regularly called her team of vendors when things went well. Her consistent, positive feedback made them eager to pick up the phone whenever they saw her number. It made her far more successful when she had to deliver hard feedback when something didn't go well for her or one of her clients.

I've since taken a page from her book. Whenever I co-facilitate a workshop with someone, my standard practice is to either meet or call them right afterward to debrief. I reach out both when things go great and when they don't. In these conversations, I always ask two simple questions:

1 What went well?
2 What could go better next time?

And because I make it a ritual, people expect the conversation, sometimes calling or reaching out to me first, and they come to the conversation already owning their part, and sometimes more. This ritual makes it easier for people to argue for responsibility rather than credit. I have found that people "tell on themselves," admitting where they could have been better or stronger. This ritual and these questions set the foundation for a safe and productive speak-up container.

For example, a co-facilitator might say, "I messed up slide seventeen."

"It's all good," I'll reassure them. "No one could tell, and we recovered beautifully. What can we do differently and better next time?"

The ritual means we're constantly trying new things and finding ways to get better, incrementally, and significantly improving along the way.

Rely on the FBI

"Good job!" "You're lazy!"

One-liners may be fine for jokes—I have attempted to crack a few thus far in this book, and you know there will be more attempts the rest of the way. But when it comes to giving and receiving feedback, one-liners are insufficient, if not detrimental.

When you do share feedback or are in a healthy environment where consistent feedback is a ritual and norm, how can you most effectively share what you have to say? Look no further than the FBI.

No, no. Not that FBI. This initialism stands for *feeling, behavior, impact*—a model of feedback I first learned in a training session led by the Chapman & Co. Leadership Institute. Yes, the same Bob Chapman referenced in chapter 7. His machinery manufacturing company has a world-class leadership training institute that teaches their own employees and clients how to hold effective feedback conversations and become better leaders and listeners. Amazing.

The FBI framework ensures your feedback is specific, real, and meaningful. The format helps you own your experience and invites another to do the same. You can use an FBI for delivering positive or constructive feedback by talking about:

- **Feeling.** This describes the emotion(s) generated in you by another's actions.

- **Behavior.** Just the facts! Behavior describes the specific events that evoked your feelings.

- **Impact.** This unpacks the effect the behavior and feeling had on you in the past, how it influences you in the present moment, and how it may affect you and them going forward.

It behooves you—especially when you start using this methodology and when you have some significant feedback to share—to write it out. Getting it down on paper can help you sort out your feelings, ideas, and words. Writing out an FBI also encourages you to look at the situation more objectively before sharing it. *Is this really what happened? Is this how I truly feel?* Something about reading your own words helps you examine if what's captured is true to you and fair for them.

Positive feedback could look like this:

I feel really supported by you [feeling] having prepared and shared all those client materials, and with great organization and detail [behavior]. Your presentation was so impressive and appreciated. I want to keep working and partnering with you [impact]. Thank you.

That kind of thorough, well-rounded feedback transforms a quick "great job!" into a true sense of appreciation for another's efforts. Without proper feedback, it's near impossible to know what earned you a "great job" and how to replicate or expand upon it. A positive FBI recognizes the other person and helps them truly feel valued and seen. The recipient knows exactly what's so great about the work they've been doing and the behavior they've displayed. They have a better idea of what to keep doing and amplify to be successful going forward. For those motivated by words of affirmation, an FBI can be a reward in and of itself.

Next up, constructive feedback:

When you were late to three client meetings last week [behavior] it made me feel frustrated, alone, and abandoned [feeling]. I'm not sure I can rely on you, with what you have on your plate right now [impact]. This isn't like you. Are you okay? [Bonus: an open-ended question meant to create dialogue.]

This statement names the feeling (simply, being let down), the behavior (lateness), and the impact (distrust and unreliability). Note that the order of the FBI doesn't matter, so long as all three components are there. And specifically with constructive feedback, it can be very valuable to end with an open-ended question to evoke dialogue. While it may be hard and uncomfortable to share and hear an FBI, it's real. It's far better than angrily labeling someone "lazy" or "irresponsible" to their face, behind their back, or not giving any feedback at all. Their behavior is not their identity. Their behavior is simply their behavior— it is information.

If you share your feedback with tact, care, respect, and the intent to start a dialogue, **the right people will be ready and willing to engage and grow.**

While it may be uncomfortable for someone to receive a constructive FBI, the recipient may build greater empathy with the person delivering it, understanding why they may be reacting in a particular way. Note, too, that sharing feelings is not about labeling the other person as irresponsible or unreliable and so on. This is about simply stating the feeling a behavior creates. And that means there's more room for the other person to respond honestly and take responsibility for their part. That's the purpose of the bonus open-ended question at the end of the constructive FBI—to give the recipient space to respond and share their experience if they're ready.

The FBI gives you a tool you can use to confront and initiate hard conversations to help one another grow. The purpose of the FBI is to start dialogue, to encourage someone to speak up and share what's going on for them. That way, you can learn more about what makes them tick, what gets in their way, and how best to support them. You can approach and work with them with greater empathy and more Platinum going forward. You may learn that they feel they have too much on their plate or have been assigned tasks they're not trained to do or may be outside their comfort zone. You may find out they're struggling at home or with a particular relationship, professional or otherwise, and it's affecting how they're performing on the job. Use the FBI to own your experience, invite others to own theirs, and open dialogue to improve and grow together, or apart, if that's what's best.

A positive FBI leaves someone knowing exactly what behavior is rewarded. A constructive FBI shares your honest experience and can start meaningful dialogue. After all, feedback, when delivered well, creates productive conversation and growth all around.

With that pattern in place, you can say "FBI," and your people will know exactly what you mean. But that doesn't mean you can just drop your feedback on their plate whenever you feel like it. That's like dropping a four-course meal in front of someone who isn't hungry. You've got to consider when your feedback will be best received. Again, more Platinum, for the win.

When—and How—Will You Be Best Heard?

The best time for your opinion to be heard, of course, is when it's asked for. So, what do you do when you have an opinion and it's not being asked for? Well, you can offer it up and see if it's both welcome and at a good time. After all, how many times have you been caught off guard by feedback or some message— personal or professional—and wished that you had received it at a different time, or in a different manner? This comes back, yet again, to the Platinum Rule, which includes knowing how and when the people around you wish to receive feedback.

You might say (or type), "FBI: Is now a good time?" This, by the way, is way better than, "Are you free? I need to have a conversation with you." Or even, "Is now a good time to talk?" As an aside, I met one young CEO, an engineer by trade, who was surprised that her subordinates freaked out when she sent them a random "Are you free to talk?" text message, even though she wanted nothing more than to genuinely check in and catch up. If you want to check in on your people and have no feedback, updates, or bad news to share, make that explicit. Otherwise, a simple check-in text can send people into a convincing tailspin—*I'm getting fired! I'm in trouble!* Building in the FBI as a ritual gives you a safer, more predictable, and consistent tool and language you can use to initiate those hard conversations without people arriving to them with their tails already between their legs. And just because you're free may not mean they are. Remember the influence you hold. They may just say they're free because the big cheese is asking.

When you ask if it's a good time for an FBI, give them a chance to respond with honesty. It might be, "I'm so sorry. I have an important meeting in a few minutes. I really want to hear what you have to say, but I know I won't be able to listen as well as I'd like to. Can we go for a walking meeting this afternoon at four o'clock instead?"

Make sure everyone's on the same page regarding cultural norms and expectations. Today, I have a small team of my own. Delivering thoughtful feedback on a regular basis, and doing so in a manner that aligns with everyone's individual preferences, is part of our values. It takes work and it's worth it. By the same token, if someone joins our team and isn't okay with giving or receiving feedback, that's on us. We've got to sort that out from the start, or even before the start. We probably shouldn't hire someone who does not want to receive or give feedback. It's part of our culture. Recall pickle theory (our environment, culture, and surroundings, or pickle brine, influence our behavior, both positively and negatively). Feedback is a key ingredient in our team's pickle brine.

If you see the merit in feedback, I encourage you to make it part of your interview and onboarding process. Ask candidates, "How do you best like to receive feedback?" If they're stumped, you can throw out a handful of options. If the answer is *E, none of the above*, they may not be a good addition to your team, or, perhaps, they have been previously burned by leaders and colleagues providing feedback in a far less refined manner than using the FBI. Alternatively, ask them about a time when they received feedback and it went well, or when they gave or received feedback and it could have gone better. Their responses will provide valuable insight into whether they're on the same page when it comes to caring personally and challenging directly, as *Radical Candor* teaches us, or if there's real potential for them to get there.

It Starts in the Mirror

FBIS are great for regular touchpoints. As your team begins to hum and chum with FBIs on the weekly, you can introduce another process on a less frequent basis—360-degree feedback: gathering more holistic and objective feedback from superiors, colleagues, direct reports, and even customers and vendors.

While there are self-assessments we can take to discover our own levels of grit, mental acuity, and resilience—Rich Diviney actually has these on his website at TheAttributes.com—there are certain things in our human experience we aren't allowed to claim about ourselves. Just as I cannot proclaim that I'm funny or good-looking, one cannot label themselves a great leader or teammate, as empathetic or a wonderful listener. Others decide that based on how they experience us and how our behavior makes them feel. If people laugh at your jokes, you're funny. If others call you a great leader or teammate, it brings far more validity and merit than decreeing yourself as such. Indeed, if you come across someone who calls themselves a great leader or teammate, feel free to run; run far away. When it comes to the designation of being a great leader or teammate, we need to hear from the perspectives and experiences of others. Three-sixty-degree feedback tools, of which there are many out there, can help a lot.

I've participated in many 360 processes, both others' and my own. They're powerful and effective for individual and team performance. Ultimately, the process allows for another avenue of regular—and in this case, more intense—insights from others. Because of how our brains are wired, no matter how hard we look in the mirror we cannot be truly objective with ourselves about our strengths, limitations, confidence, arrogance, or insecurities. As a friend of mine likes to say, it's very hard to read the label on the jar when you're stuck inside the jar. Feedback from others is a better mirror, one that gives us truer, greater awareness of how we show up, how we impact others, and how we can keep getting better. It is even more powerful to be able to debrief one's 360 results with a coach and, if you're ready and willing, your own team.

One of the best ways you can grow is to hear honest feedback from the people who work with you consistently. You are not allowed to label yourself a good leader or teammate—only your team can do that. And it's not a permanent designation, either. You earn it (or diminish it) with every move you make.

Don't Just Dish It Out, Receive It Too

That brings us to a key tenet of a healthy feedback culture. If you want to be a great leader, you can't just dish out feedback; you must create the condition to receive it and seek it out as well. The whole point of feedback is that it is designed to be shared, to be mutual, and to create dialogue that leads to improved relationships and growth. And the greatest leaders among us invite feedback just as much as, if not more than, they dish it out.

You can even keep a tally, tracking your ratio of feedback given to feedback received. I think that ratio should be pretty darn close to one-to-one, and that's hard to do when you're in a position of leadership. In that role, it's far easier to dish it out than it is to solicit and receive it.

After delivering an FBI, you can invite the other person to share their experience of you with you. Of course, in the vein of "encourage and reward," you must reward people when they do. If you defend, make them wrong, or attempt to explain yourself, you may just be shutting them down. Say thank you, ask for clarification if needed, and, if the feedback is constructive, ask what they feel you could do to improve. You don't have to agree with it, but you ought to respect it, or find some merit in the feedback, if you ever want to hear more of it.

One boss I had came nowhere near a one-to-one ratio with feedback. It felt much closer to twenty-to-one of feedback given to me versus feedback received by them. And that assessment may be generous. Even worse, nearly all the feedback given to me was negative, delivered at their convenience, often without request or warning, and offered as if it were a matter of fact, without assuming any positive intent from me and without room for or interest in my perspective. Yuck. I felt like a punching bag. I share this with you to emphasize that the purpose of feedback is not to reprimand but to build relationship, open dialogue with others, and seek to understand each other's perspectives, experiences, strengths, limitations, and gaps. The purpose of feedback is to help one another grow, not knock each other down.

So, how do you know if you're on the right track when it comes to sharing feedback? My mother-in-law, who was an excellent elementary school teacher (and I'll admit, I'm biased), shared an important lesson with me on this front, something she remembered learning at teacher's college decades ago. If two or more students in your class aren't learning something after repeated attempts, it could have something to do with your approach. In other words, if your students (or team or employees or culture) are struggling, it behooves you to look in the mirror! You may just be the only thing in common in all your failing relationships. Feel free to read that sentence again. It means it's likely time to taste your own dish and examine if your approach is working. If it's not and you don't know what to change, ask for help. Gain from the perspective of another colleague, or even ask your team what's working and not working for them. Then truly listen.

Remember the Platinum Rule. Your feedback shared with others ought to consider how and when they wish to receive feedback, not simply your own preferences. Ask yourself if you're doing something to enable behaviors and consider whether a system or process may be getting in the way. If you're still stuck, think about how you can avoid repeating conversations you've already had. Switching things up may start a new kind of dialogue. Genuinely asking your people what they need may help too.

You can invite your team to share their feedback. You might provide options for sharing anonymous feedback, along with prompting people with quantitative options (e.g., On a scale of zero to ten, how valuable was my presentation?) versus soliciting only qualitative ones. Feel free to get creative, and keep in mind that as the leader, you often must make the first move. You set the tone. Vulnerability is contagious.

Again, when someone bravely offers their opinion and feedback to you, choose your response wisely. If you shut them down, defend yourself, make them wrong, or make yourself right, that may be the last honest feedback you ever hear.

Just as feedback can't be unilaterally "right," it can't be "wrong" either. While you're allowed to ask follow-up questions, seek to understand. Make sure you're not gaslighting them or negating what has likely taken a good amount of courage to share. And if you're not in the right place physically or emotionally to receive the feedback, let them know—for example: "I value what you have to share, and I truly want to be able to hear it. Can we have this conversation this afternoon instead?" And under no circumstances should you sit on the feedback you have for them so that you can turn the tables when they share something with you.

In truth, though, it can be harder to give feedback than it is to receive. A *Harvard Business Review* article shared survey results that 44 percent of managers agreed that giving criticism was stressful or difficult, and 21 percent admitted that they avoid it. Particularly in the context of the Great Resignation, I've met numerous leaders who worry that having hard conversations will cause their best people to head for the hills. So many people have asked me, "What if I give them critical feedback and they quit?" "Well," I typically respond, "what if you don't give them feedback and they *stay?*"

If you share your feedback with tact, care, respect, and the intent to start a dialogue, the right people will be ready and willing to engage and grow. Think back to the leaders who affected your life. They're often the ones who gave critical feedback and helped you grow, not the ones who let you coast. And if you've embraced what we've discussed so far when it comes to leadership, you'll be on your way to cultivating a culture where feedback is experienced as a gift rather than an attack.

10

What's Really at Stake?

"In recognizing the humanity of our fellow beings, we pay ourselves the highest tribute."
THURGOOD MARSHALL

WE BEGAN this book with the life-and-death consequences of failing to foster a speak-up culture. What's really at stake isn't only our bottom line or the safety of our operations for employees and customers. What's truly at stake is our humanity. And to preserve it for everyone we serve, internal and external to our organizations and society at large, we must ensure we are open to and in search of experiences, perspectives, and opinions that differ from our own. A speak-up culture is a requisite for such endeavors. Indeed, when the human in us sees the human in others, we progress.

Listen So Others May Speak

Juliana Tafur is a documentary filmmaker and entrepreneur, among other things, who draws on psychology and art to help people better understand each other. Her award-winning film, *List(e)n*, documented three conversations, each between two people with opposing viewpoints, on hot button US political issues: guns, abortion, and immigration. The subjects of her film were invited simply to listen to each other.

In conversation, Tafur shared with me a significant motivator for the participants—they were promised they would be able to share their point of view. Each person saw it as a platform from which to convince others—mainly viewers—that their perspective was right.

Through a series of question prompts and exercises that Tafur and her team provided as guidance, the participants began sharing. Two of the three pairs formed a genuine connection with each other. They were surprised by how much they could at least understand the other's point of view, even though they didn't agree with each other's stance. Some found themselves in tears, and two out of three pairs walked away as new friends.

Interestingly, the pair that clashed talked about immigration. Both participants had immigration in their background. One was a first-generation immigrant who was vehemently opposed to immigration reform and accused his counterpart of being "not a true American."

While this conversation was abruptly shut down by one participant, the other two are nothing short of inspiring. And all three conversations are fascinating and telling. The documentary is beautiful and provides hope for humanity in our ability to work through and see beyond our differences, and to find common ground.

Tafur's experiment is proof that, in many scenarios, if we seek to understand each other and find validity in someone else's point of view—to establish speak-up cultures in our interpersonal relationships, organizations, and communities—we can foster more connection and unity and limit division and oppression. Sign. Me. Up.

However, confronting the hardest conversations about our own identities is not how most of us approach our differences. Think about the traditional conventions of a good old holiday family dinner. Some families intentionally avoid controversial topics that may cause discomfort, disagreement, and argument. Conversations about politics, religion, sexual orientation, gender identity, gender equality, racial equality, Indigenous rights, and the like are often contentious or verboten. Wouldn't it be nice if we all had permission and the right attitudes and skill sets for meaningful dialogue that ends in greater understanding, much like what occurred in two of three conversations in *List(e)n*?

At work, "speak-up cultures" and "psychological safety" have entered the vernacular. As a result, numerous leaders claim they want this type of culture. But in reality, they may simply feel pressure to make it so—much like the pressure we feel to attend those holiday family dinners. Or, they may simply wish to reap the benefits of hearing people's ideas to make the operation more successful. So, they say to their teams that they want to hear their people's ideas, concerns, disagreements, and mistakes. But do they really? And are they truly equipped to handle what may come their way?

Often, when their teams take their word for it and open up—sharing what's really on their minds or asking for policy changes that reflect true self-expression—those leaders realize things felt a whole lot easier for them when the culture was more "We Don't Talk about Bruno" and less "Let It Go." (That's a reference for all you Disney fans out there.) However, the true test of whether you have a speak-up culture is whether people feel comfortable behaving as they authentically are and sharing their truth. Yes, with tact, respect, and decorum, but not a truth filter.

Can people wear their hair naturally or show their tattoos and piercings? Can they talk about pay equity and the experiences of marginalized populations at work and beyond? Can they discuss pressing issues like gun reform and *Roe v. Wade*?

One company, Basecamp, announced in April 2021 that there would be "no more societal and political discussions on our company Basecamp account." Shortly thereafter, around one-third of its employees resigned, and CEO Jason Fried apologized. Demanding that your people keep the issues that affect them away from the confines of their work (in office, virtually, or otherwise) will most likely create a more silent and homogeneous workforce, possibly one ridden with toxic positivity. It also isn't a fair standard. To expect your people to leave their lives at home is inconsistent with our human experience. Life bleeds into work and vice versa. And those of us who work from home are likely to feel that more than ever.

Although I'm a believer in being professional and having appropriate context as part of one's vulnerability, expecting people to separate life from work is, in my opinion, antiquated. If you want a healthy and thriving speak-up culture, it may even include employee activism. After all, if leaders set a psychologically safe speak-up culture as the goal, they are going to hear about what employees want for their lives and in society at large. Thinking that organizations, especially companies, can help us progress on some of society's biggest issues is reasonable; in fact, we should expect it. One of my favorite quotes comes from Margaret Mead: "Never doubt that a small group of thoughtful, committed citizens can change the world; indeed, it's the only thing that ever has."

Business should drive, innovate, lead, and support changes in humanity and society for the better. Standing for something bigger than profit is also an advantage in breeding genuine employee and customer loyalty.

Honoring Visible and Invisible Diversity

Research and experience have shown us that diversity, some of which can't be seen, is hugely beneficial to business. Take neurodiversity, a term used to describe a variety of conditions related to cognitive abilities. It applies to conditions such as autism spectrum disorder (ASD), dyslexia, dyscalculia (difficulty learning and performing arithmetic), attention deficit hyperactivity disorder (ADHD), and obsessive-compulsive disorder (OCD). Friends, family members, and colleagues may be neurodivergent without you, or even them, knowing. This was the case for Nate Swann.

Swann was an army aviation officer flying aircraft, including some of the most advanced helicopters in the world, with the 160th Special Operations Aviation Regiment. He had the chance to take special mission operators to some of the deepest, darkest places around the globe, and to fly airplanes at high altitudes doing reconnaissance missions. In roles that required him to be available at all hours, he led organizations of more than five hundred people. And all those career highlights never would have been possible if he had walked into the US Army at age eighteen with the neurodivergent diagnosis he came to have.

In fact, he lived thirty-six years without ever knowing that he was neurodivergent. Fourteen years into a successful career as a junior officer and mid-grade senior officer, several factors collided. He moved into a new position in a new area and became a parent at the same time. Shortly after, all those changes came to a head. After a rough morning, in an outsized reaction to the conversation they were having, he ended up yelling at several of his superiors and colleagues over videoconference. He was thrown out of the meeting.

While he didn't know exactly what was going on, Swann knew something wasn't right. So, he went to see his unit's aeromedical psychologist. He was speaking about a mile a minute as he described what had been happening. "Am I going crazy?" he asked. "Is this early-onset Alzheimer's or something?"

The psychologist looked at him quizzically. "Do you always talk this fast?" she asked.

Taken aback by the question, he replied, "Um, yes. In my family we call it 'Swann squawk.' It's just how we talk. Whoever talks the loudest and the fastest gets heard."

"Hmm, that's interesting," she replied. "Have you ever been diagnosed with ADHD?"

Swann laughed at the notion. "Well, of course not. I'm a pilot," he responded. As of this writing, ADHD is a disqualifier for both civil and military aviation.

Over the next few months, they discovered that Swann did have some differences in terms of how he processed and saw the world. In 2018, he was diagnosed with ADHD, and two years later, he was diagnosed with Asperger's syndrome, a form of autism. If those diagnoses had come during childhood, he would have had a very different life and would not have been able to influence the world the way he has, at least not with the US military under present-day standards. There is most definitely a time and place for diagnoses and early intervention, but in Swann's case, the diagnoses would have blockaded his chosen career path.

That is something he believes we need to solve for going forward. Especially since, as he says, "the reality is, neurodiversity affects everyone, and if you can get to the heart of the neurodiversity conversation, and focus organizations, cultures, and leadership on how people interact with the world, we can achieve a lot more inside the organization without a whole lot of change. Because we're focusing on what individuals need. And when we do it for those people, you get a snowball effect." He continues, "Not only do you realize benefits for those who are neurotypical and those who are neurodivergent, but for leaders themselves, who get a chance to learn about how *they* interact with the world." Swann believes that if everyone could view the world through "the lens of neurodiversity," humanity would be not just more inclusive, but also more capable of seeing beyond each other's differences and leveraging the wide array of talents and perspectives everyone has to offer.

Hiren Shukla is similarly passionate about supporting a neurodiverse workforce, and he and Swann collaborate on their efforts. As founder and leader of Ernst & Young's Neurodiversity Centres of Excellence, Shukla is responsible for converting the organization's neurodiversity inclusiveness effort into exceptional client service and tangible ROI. While Shukla identifies as neurotypical, he knows a thing or two about not belonging. Shukla is an Indian who was born and raised in East Africa. His family of seven fled genocide and landed in the melting pot that is New York City. His language dialect was both Indian and East African. He lived in India for five years and didn't feel he fit in. He lived in Texas for some time and didn't feel he fit in. He's familiar with the feeling of suppressing one's own identity to get by.

"You've heard the phrase, 'Bring your whole self to work.' Well, when I bring my whole self to work, there's a lot of baggage that comes with it," Shukla shares. "When people have the space to feel safe and supported in truly bringing their whole selves to work, they'll innovate from the same place."

That kind of thinking inspired Shukla to establish the first Neurodiversity Centre of Excellence, and since then, they have helped sixty-five and counting other organizations move forward with similar initiatives. As he explains, "If we allow individuals to feel safe, we will unlock value that is sitting under our noses."

When we find ways to be more inclusive of those who are neurodivergent—a difference that is often invisible—we can create more diverse, equitable, and inclusive cultures and organizations entirely. When we embrace different perspectives, we

Seeing the humanity in one another is the only way to achieve the kind of progress we wish to see in both business and our society at large.

have a more holistic view, and that means we can better include and serve more people internally and externally. That typically means better and more resilient results.

Importantly, Shukla says, "it is up to organizations and leaders to make us feel we belong." If we don't, we're far less likely to have a speak-up culture. And if we want to stick around, both in our roles and on this planet, we don't have a choice.

In an ahead-of-its-time stand-up comedy bit from 1992, George Carlin discusses humanity's concern for the plight of Earth. He explains that while we're worried about saving the whales, the snails, and the planet, it's us—the people—we should be concerned about. "The planet is fine," Carlin exclaims. "The people are [expletive]!" While the planet will likely survive, at least until everything in our known universe is pulled into a black hole (well, that got dark real quick), our days of thriving on this planet are being challenged and limited, expedited by our own behavior. As a species, we aren't owners, we're renters. And not great ones at that.

What's our best option to hopefully lengthen our stay here or successfully transition to settling and thriving elsewhere off Earth? Cooperation: to learn to care more about each other and seek to see and appreciate another's perspective—much as Juliana Tafur's work helps us do—by truly listening to one another and our various points of view. Again, we don't have to agree with someone to listen, respect them, seek to understand, and truly make progress. This requires us to show up with humility and to own our mistakes and shortcomings.

Own Your Impact, Intended or Not

Near the beginning of the COVID-19 pandemic, an executive director of a not-for-profit organization (aside: a mentor of mine calls them "for-impact organizations," which I love and much prefer) asked me to speak with his team virtually, as their organization was pivoting to entirely online working and offerings. It was a challenging time full of change and uncertainty for the team, as it was for all of us. I had been involved with the organization, volunteering in various capacities, over many years. I was happy to join them and share any insight I could to help.

The virtual session began, and I shared a couple ideas about successfully pivoting, which literally means to move around a central axis. Imagine a basketball player planting their pivot foot and then moving the other foot around it. When it comes to individuals, teams, and organizations, pivoting means you keep your purpose and cause intact and pivot around it to bring it to life in new ways, given the context.

After these and a few other opening remarks about pivoting and change, we moved into a Q&A discussion. Everything seemed to be going fine, even well. A team member I had known for many years asked the next question about how to move forward under a particular set of challenging circumstances, and part of my response included a comment on optimally performing and highly trusting teams. "We suffer alone, but we can struggle together," I remarked. She nodded pensively.

What I meant by that statement is that if we're in a healthy community of peers and a trusted team, and we vulnerably admit struggle, then others will come to our aid. Meanwhile, if we struggle in silence, it can quickly turn into suffering. If people don't know we're struggling, how do they know to help? But not everyone participating in the virtual session received it that way.

Just by looking around at the faces on the screen in front of me, I could tell that something I said hadn't landed the way I had intended. At that moment, I had a choice. I could charge forward, satisfied with the response from the person who asked the question, and ignore what I had just noticed. Or I could pause and ask for others' perspectives. "I feel like I just said something that didn't sit right with everyone. Would anyone like to share?" I asked. And they did.

"What about oppressed populations?" someone passionately spoke up. "Some people don't feel safe to 'struggle together.' Some people aren't ever given that option."

Several people on the team were of marginalized identities, and they thought my statement was inconsiderate, narrow-minded, and privileged. Of course, that's not who I wanted to be or how I wanted to be perceived. Now I had another choice. I could shut them down, explaining that they misheard or misunderstood me. Or I could say, "I've upset you, and while it wasn't my intention, it's still happened. Please, are you willing to tell me more?" Fortunately, I went with the latter.

Afterward, during a debrief call, the executive director apologized for some of the team challenging me.

"Don't," I said. "That was completely fair game and a great learning opportunity for me. In fact, it's a testament to the speak-up culture present on your team." I was truly glad the team had challenged me on my perspective. I hadn't meant to offend anyone, of course, but I left that call with greater awareness of my words and perspectives. It was a growing experience for me. While I was challenged and even called out, I was given an opportunity and chose to be called in—to learn, be human, connect with others meaningfully, and improve. Was it a curveball? Absolutely. But it led to a healthy, safe, and worthwhile conversation that ought to have happened. And in the days, weeks, and months after, the executive director gave me positive feedback: the conversation continued to be great for the team's cohesion and the organizational culture.

What I've learned and work very hard to embody is that good leaders own their impact on others, whether it is intended or not. An insecure leader will complain, "That's not what I meant!"

A secure leader will request, "Please tell me more. I didn't intend to, but still, I've hurt you. I truly wish to hear more so I can do better by you and others to follow."

Less Sympathy, More Empathy

A speak-up culture requires us to believe that all people deserve dignity. And while it's fine to maintain a certain perspective or set of beliefs, if you truly wish to cultivate an inclusive speak-up culture, you must examine your perspectives, beliefs, and actions deeply if they inhibit someone else's ability to exist on their own terms. As author and activist Robert Jones Jr. (aka Son of Baldwin) said, "We can disagree and still love each other unless your disagreement is rooted in my oppression and denial of my humanity and right to exist." Sometimes, that requires an uncomfortable—or even painful—reckoning with who we are, how we show up, and how we ought to change.

As we talk about the differences inherent in our lives and the lives of others, it's important to touch on empathy as opposed to sympathy. As Brené Brown so articulately explains, "Empathy fuels connection. Sympathy drives disconnection." In a short video, Brown shares the four qualities of empathy laid out by Theresa Wiseman, a nursing scholar who studied empathy-driven professions. Empathy involves perspective-taking, non-judgment, recognizing others' emotions, and communicating that recognition. "Empathy is feeling *with* people," Brown says. "I always think of empathy as this kind of sacred space where someone's in a deep hole, and they shout from the bottom, 'I'm stuck. It's dark. I'm overwhelmed.' In response, we climb down and say, 'Hey! I know what it's like down here, and you're not alone.'"

Meanwhile, sympathy is when we look down into that hole and decide to stay right where we are. While we may feel sorry for another, we seldom connect. In the video, Brown explains, "Empathy is a choice and it's a vulnerable choice, because to connect with you I have to connect with something in myself that knows that feeling."

While we may not be able to relate to others' experiences and emotions, we can always seek to understand, care, and help. This is what's called cognitive empathy, rather than emotional empathy. After all, as Brown says, "The truth is, rarely can a response make something better. What makes something better is connection."

And that connection can be forged, even under the most extreme circumstances. Activist and Emmy- and Peabody Award–winning filmmaker Deeyah Khan has discovered this time and time again. For one film project, *White Right: Meeting the Enemy*, she decided to meet with violent white supremacists who believe their race is under threat. She wanted to understand their perspective and why their lives had been consumed by such hatred. She found that her own beliefs were tested by the experiment, as were those of the people she spoke to.

So often, the people we think we "hate" are those with whom we have no relationship. After she spent considerable time with the largest neo-Nazi organization in the United States, three of the movement's leaders chose to leave the organization, crediting their conversations with Khan for the decision. As a Muslim woman, Khan represented much of what these white supremacists hated in the world. When she formed a meaningful connection and even a caring friendship with these people, they had a crisis of identity. The woman they were supposed to hate formed more of a caring connection with them than some of the people they were bonded to in their own group—people they would call brother or sister.

Although this is an extreme example, it's proof that to do the work of improving humanity and organizational culture, we must approach others with empathy and compassion.

I'll admit that I'm still learning and will always be learning about diversity, equity, inclusion, and belonging. I am aware that I was born with much wind at my back, with the privilege of being a white man from an upper-middle-class family. I've learned more about privilege and oppression in recent years than ever before due to current events regarding ongoing issues of gender inequality, racism, equity, and LGBTQ2S+ and Indigenous rights. I've committed to address any bias within me that rears its head, especially if it's uncomfortable. All of us are charged with addressing the thoughts, feelings, and behaviors counter to who we say we are and what we say we care about—this is part of the say-do gap that authentic and humble leaders work to close. It's impossible to remove bias completely. But we can build awareness of our biases and judgments and discern if they represent our values—who we strive to be at our best—and respond accordingly. I have come to believe that the responsibility of privilege is to lift others up, even if it costs you your own privilege.

Ultimately, between our values and behaviors is choice. If the way we act doesn't align with a deeply held value and belief we hold, we've got some work to do. As author Stephen Covey paraphrased, "Between stimulus and response, there is a space. In that space is our power to choose our response. In our response lies our growth and our freedom."

It's up to us to see the humanity in one another. In many ways, it's the only way to achieve the kind of progress we wish to see in both business and our society at large.

11

It's Personal

*"I think fearless is having
fears but jumping anyway."*
TAYLOR SWIFT

'D **LIKE** to share one last vital idea.

As you embark on the work of building a speak-up culture within your organization, team, and life, you must recognize that leadership is personal—it must be. Those who feel called to lead—who do it out of a deep sense of responsibility and not for the ego boost and attention—care personally about the work they are doing and the people they serve.

This work of cultivating speak-up cultures is personal to me because I know what it feels like to be voiceless. And I'm a big believer that, often, our greatest strengths and purpose are closely tied to our biggest challenges, hardships, and even traumas. On the other side of our struggle can be passion, and so often, our purpose lives in helping others join us on the other side.

Feeling Voiceless

Stuttering is hereditary. It typically affects males more than females, and the Shedletzky men have struggled with stuttering and stammering for generations. I love and respect my lineage, but this inheritance has brought much challenge in my life, along with triumph. In second grade, I learned I wouldn't be an exception to the hereditary rule.

If you catch it early—before a child is aware of their stutter—and introduce various therapies, the stutter can improve without incident. But once a child realizes that they have a speech impediment, things can become a whole lot trickier. While we don't quite understand the physiology that causes a stutter, we now know that psychology can have a tremendous impact on one's ability to improve it. When a person knows they are stuttering, it becomes much harder to address it. But we didn't necessarily have that insight in the mid-nineties when I was in primary school.

Back then, at the age of seven, my first speech therapist handed me a clicker and instructed me to count the number of times I stuttered in a day. The idea was that if I were more aware of my stutters, I would slow down and speak more clearly. But instead, I became hyper-fixated on the behavior I wished to eradicate. And I didn't want to explain myself to the other kids, either.

I distinctly remember the first (and only) day I took that clicker to school. It felt heavy in my palm as my mom drove me and a group of carpool kids to school that morning. *What the heck am I going to do with this thing?* I wondered, staring at it. I stuffed it into my school bag. Two hours later, I found out. We had recess at 10:15 that morning. I decided to be an obedient boy and brought my clicker outside. While playing, I stuttered once, pulled it out of my pocket, and clicked it.

"What are you doing?" a kid asked.

"I don't know," I replied, shoving it into my pocket. And that was the end of that. After school that day, the clicker was firmly planted in the desk drawer of my room, and there it stayed.

I successfully did nothing for four years. My stutter wasn't awful, but it certainly affected my confidence and made me less willing to speak up in class and among my peers. It wasn't until sixth-grade French class, when I experienced one of the most embarrassing moments of my life, that I knew I needed to do more, and something different.

The teacher, Madame Vieux, distributed a stapled printout in French and explained that each student would take a turn reading aloud from it. I was sitting in the back right corner of the classroom, in the second to last row. As the line of readers snaked toward me, I could feel my heartbeat pick up. Not only would I have to speak publicly; I'd have to do it in a language that wasn't my mother tongue. As the person before me began reading, I scanned the paragraph that I thought would be mine, looking to see which words I might have trouble with.

Time ran out; I was nervous as heck, and I began reading. It was going well enough—at least until I got to the word *très*. *Très*, likely the third freaking word you learn in French! The harsh beginning of the word was a sound I struggled with, and that day was no exception. I couldn't do it. The harder I tried to force it out, the harder it became—like a finger trap. After repeated attempts to force the word out of my mouth, I paused as if to give myself a break before trying again, and Madame gave me a look.

"*Stephen, quel est le problème?*" she asked. "Stephen, what is the problem?"

Frightened, I stared down at the page and attempted to push out the word once more. I couldn't do it. It was agonizing. I gave up.

"I can't pronounce the word," I finally submitted.

"You can't pronounce *très?*" Madame Vieux asked, incredulously.

I shook my head.

"*Au suivant!* Next!" she said, moving right past me.

To say I felt dejected would be an understatement. When class ended, I approached her desk and tried to explain what had happened. "I have a stutter," I said. She shrugged, clearly uninterested and still peeved at me that I couldn't—or, in her mind, perhaps chose not to—pronounce *très*. While I didn't like the way I felt or was treated, I'm thankful Madame Vieux gave me this kick in the behind. I realized that if I didn't get a grip on it, my stutter would hold me back for the rest of my life. I went home from school that day and told my mom what had happened. I was determined to get help.

That summer, I found myself at the Speech and Stuttering Institute's summer program in downtown Toronto. At thirteen, I was the youngest person there. One other participant, a man in his mid-twenties, was highly educated, but because he couldn't speak at job interviews—his stutter got in the way—he hadn't been able to land a job. Another, an older teenager of Sri Lankan descent named George, couldn't pronounce his own last name. We spent an entire session one day helping him sound out every syllable. It was the first time in his entire life that he uttered his own last name. It was both a painful series of minutes and a kind of beautiful victory at the same time. Our speech therapist, the late and brilliant Dr. Robert (Bob) Kroll, did such a marvelous job facilitating this exercise with this young man, exuding such patience, safety, and grace. The way he acknowledged George for completing the task in the end generated a heart-warming and palpable pride in both George and the entire group.

A few important things happened to me in that program. First, I realized that it wasn't too late for me. In fact, this was a fairly early intervention. *Phew.* Second, I was fortunate not to have a severe stutter. While this gave me mixed feelings—a bit of guilt that I had it easier than some—it instilled relief, hope, and some confidence and personal agency as well. And third, I could be of service. I began to help others with their speech-related struggles. Not overly intentionally, it just kind of happened. And because I'm human, it felt good, and I wanted to keep doing it. In particular, I befriended the job seeker in his mid-twenties as if I were his little brother. I felt as though I was helping him build his confidence and strategies to overcome his stutter and land a job. Sharing crib notes, if you will. That feeling of helping someone along was incredible.

The program was literally a life changer for me. I gained confidence and tools, and Dr. Kroll also began my education on how to be an excellent and caring facilitator.

The next summer, I was back to my regularly scheduled programming. I was at another summer camp, but without a speech therapy focus this time around. With newfound confidence, I was cast to participate in a theater performance. It was a sketch comedy–style show, and I was playing a character who had a complicated last name. The day of the production, the staff chose me and a few peers to make a quick announcement about the performance that evening, inviting the whole camp to attend. We devised our skit on the spot and as we practiced on the lawn next to the dining hall, I fumbled and couldn't pronounce the last name of my character. My peers and the staff member with us didn't know what had gotten into me. I was nervous. There were 450 people in the dining hall where we were to perform our little skit.

But I swallowed and pressed on. In character, I attempted to introduce myself, and my worst nightmare transpired. I stuttered. One, two, three attempts before I could get out the name in full. With the name hanging in the air, I glanced around, my palms sweating, heart racing, face flushing. And either nobody noticed or nobody cared. It was one of the most liberating feelings of my life. My worst fear had been realized, and I didn't die. In fact, nothing bad happened at all.

Feeling a sense of relief, I went on to do the production that night, which went off without a hitch. I was in several scenes, including a singing parody to the tune of "Singing in the Rain." I got laughs, and I had an absolute blast. I remember a shared feeling of elation with everyone involved in the production afterward. It was a true highlight. For those moments, I felt on top of the world.

Most importantly, I learned that one of the best ways to overcome my fear was consistent exposure. I had to get up in front of people, or have conversations with friends and strangers, or participate in something more important than me. And whenever I did, I realized I had something worthwhile to experience or share.

Knowing that feeling of voicelessness so intimately laid the path to my passion—helping others find their voice and feel confident enough to share it too.

Answering the Call

Those lessons about speaking up and its opportunities and consequences became that much more apparent as I got older. At work, I've been in what felt like some the safest of relationships and speak-up cultures, where there is psychological safety, a feeling that it's worth it to share, and an investment in individual and collective progress. It's truly the bee's knees. Information flows, trust builds, genuine friendships form, love for each other and the work grows, and innovation can result.

I've also been in environments where sharing is encouraged— but only if you share what senior leaders want to hear. Politics and egos get in the way; one's truth is discouraged. The more you put out there, the more trouble you seemingly get into. I've been in organizations where mistakes are swept under the rug for fear of retribution—where the culture is unhealthy, unproductive, and toxic. I've withheld information and seen others do the same because speaking up is psychologically dangerous and simply not worth it. Fear and apathy together again.

I've taken up this work because I know how good it feels to be part of a speak-up culture, both personally and professionally. I know that it enhances trust, cooperation, innovation, our health, and more. And I know that the alternative is harmful for personal and organizational health, affecting both for the worse.

This book—and this work—is personal to me, a manifestation of my approach to leadership and what I want to put out into, and see more of in, our world. If you are to take up the charge of building a speak-up culture in the environments where you have influence—at home, at work, and beyond—it must be personal to you too.

Thriving Is a High-Stakes Game

I won't lie to you: the work of building a speak-up culture can be hard, messy, imperfect, human, and scary. But remember that there is no such thing as a fearless leader. Leaders feel the fear and do it anyway. They feel connected to something bigger than themselves that makes any fear worth it. Indeed, if it weren't for fear, we would have no need for courage.

Rather than taking fear as a signal to back down, leaders take it as data suggesting that the issues at hand matter, a lot. That our ability to thrive, as individuals and as a group, is a high-stakes issue. Knowing what matters is a gateway to our own courage.

Any journey worth
going on is **made better**
when it's shared.

Our approach matters a lot. We discussed the fact that our relationship with our boss has more influence on our health than that of our relationship with our family doctor or therapist. Its impact is on par with that of our relationship with a spouse or life partner. If you have a leadership role, you directly impact your people's livelihood and well-being. How could the stakes be any higher?

Remember Why You Are Here

I've said it before, and I'll say it again: The two most powerful forces in humanity that I'm aware of are hope and each other. If you have hope, if you can see the light at the end of the tunnel—or at least know that there's light somewhere out there even if you can't see it yet—you can keep moving forward. If you lose hope, please call a friend who can remind you of why you're here and that you matter. Or better yet, call a friend and simply tell them why they matter. Gratitude, appreciation, and service to others are positively contagious.

As humans, we aren't designed to go it alone. We are social animals. As individuals, we can be good, but together we're remarkable. Any journey worth going on is made better when it's shared.

As a leader, the task of caring for those in your charge lies with you. I hope that what we have covered in these pages will help you usher in your own transformation and development and, perhaps, help others do the same. I hope it will inspire you to fear less, because you have a cause worthy of the risk. I hope it will drive you to act, because you have the tools and community to do so. And I hope it will push you to keep going—especially when the going gets tough—because what you're doing and who you are matters.

So, let me ask you:

- What matters to you?

- What makes leadership personal for you?

- What's worth pushing through the fear to get to a new and better reality in your organization, team, family, society, and beyond?

I can all but guarantee that if it has the potential to improve people's lives, it will be well worth the effort.

So please: go forth, speak up, and create the conditions to make it safe and worth it for others to do the same.

Acknowledgments

IF **YOU'RE** familiar with Gretchen Rubin's *Four Tendencies*, which I mentioned in chapter 6 and highly recommend (the book and the quiz), you'll know of the four personality categories: Upholder, Questioner, Obliger, and Rebel. I identify as a Rebel, whose tagline is, "You can't make me, and neither can I."

I remember sitting on the couch with my beloved wife one night in the early summer of 2021, after we had put our two young kids to bed. I shared my idea and impulse: "I think I'm going to write a book." Knowing my Rebel tendency better than anyone—with my propensity to procrastinate doing the hard things—my wife smartly advised against it. I'd be lying if I said that didn't provide some initial motivation to prove her (or, perhaps, myself) wrong. But Julie has been a rock, cheerleader, sounding board, grammar corrector, and idea improver all along (in fact, she corrected this very sentence!). Better than all of this, she is the absolute ideal partner in practicing the very concepts cast within this book. We work hard to build and maintain a speak-up relationship among us, our children, family, and friends. I love you, Jules. Thank you for holding and creating the space for me to pour my everything into this book.

I wrote this book, in large part, for my children, Sophie and Jack. When my kids get their first job, I want them to work *with* a leader and not *for* a driver. I want them to love what they do, why they do it, and who they get to do it with. I hope my words here contribute toward a world where leadership is better defined and more people in positions of authority behave as leaders. And I hope this book makes my kids proud.

The saying goes that it takes a village to raise a child, and the same has been true for my process with this book. This village includes many, including Julie and our kids. It also includes the amazing team at Page Two.

I met Page Two author and my mentor Liane Davey for our annual tea and catch-up. I shared my book idea with her, and later that morning an email introduction was sent to Jesse Finkelstein, cofounder and principal of Page Two. What has transpired has become a truly amazing and close friendship with Jesse and an absolute love of working with her and the world-class team at Page Two. Jesse is honest and generous and is the epitome of possessing a service orientation. Thank you for always having my back and best interest at heart and in mind, Fink.

Kendra Ward, as editorial director at Page Two, is the guardian angel of this book. To say it has been a joy to work with you on this book would be a gross understatement. You get this content, you care about this content, and you are a shining example of a speak-up leader. Thank you for your partnership, care, and guidance in making this book what it is. I am eternally grateful for you.

The rock star team of Caela Moffet as project manager; Peter Cocking and Fiona Lee as designers; Steph Vander-Meulen as copyeditor; Alison Strobel as proofreader; Chris Brandt, Meghan O'Neill, Ariel Hudnall, and Leonni Antono in marketing; Lorraine Toor, Madelaine Manson, and Colin Rier in sales; and Madison Taylor in PR has been nothing short of an author's dream. Your consistent support, guidance, enthusiasm, and sense of humor have made me better, wiser, calmer, and more confident, and have motivated me to keep going. Thank you! I feel so truly blessed to have had this experience with Page Two.

When I chose to explore writing this book, one of my first calls was to Bryan Wish, founder of Arcbound. Bryan and his team have been amazing sounding boards, connectors, supporters, and cheerleaders. Specifically, if it weren't for Ariel Hubbard, this book simply wouldn't exist—she helped bring it to life. While I'd written articles and single chapters before, I'd never constructed a book. Quite frankly, I didn't know where to start, and blank pages intimidate me. Ariel's research and writing support laid the scaffolding (and then some) for this book. Ariel, you were vital in bringing my vision for this book to life. I'm forever grateful for you, our partnership, and our work together.

Early readers also provided valuable feedback. Thank you for going above and beyond, Mark Green, Colin Fleming, and Sukie Ewald. As well, to Susan Liebel for your detailed grammar and punctuation check—a labor of love.

There are some people in our lives and careers whom we're not quite sure we deserve. This is how I feel about my dear friend and business partner, Alejandro Stevens. His research, feedback, and attention to every detail helped make this book what it is. Among countless other contributions, he helped refine the culture equation and the correlation of safety and impact forming a speak-up culture. Ale, thank you for going headfirst into too many rabbit holes. Your care, support, and service orientation are incomparable. Thank you for your undying love, care, and support of our work and relationship. Thank you for reading every single word and ensuring that each one reflected what we meant to say. Thank you for your partnership, brother.

The ideas within this book stand upon the shoulders of greats—humble giants. Scholar Amy C. Edmondson's groundbreaking work on psychological safety was the impetus, inspiration, and significant foundation of this work. I have such great respect for Amy as a person—she is a lifelong learner and giver, and she continues to make ongoing contributions to the field of leadership, management, and organizational culture. Even though I feel I am not deserving, Amy, you have embraced me as a colleague. I am forever grateful for you and your work, and I'm humbled by your support.

Speaking of another who walks their talk, I first learned of Amy's work from Adam Grant's brilliant book *Give and Take: Why Helping Others Drives Our Success*. Adam's *WorkLife*–TED podcast episode on speak-up cultures was a huge inspiration and spark for this book. Adam has been a kind and gracious supporter of my research and work from afar, sharing the contributions of many others as I've attempted to form the best possible understanding and depiction of the latest research on employee voice.

I must also thank other scholars and professionals in the field of organizational behavior: longtime friend Kyle Brykman for his support, enthusiasm, and shared resources and ideas; and Ethan Burris and Jim Detert for their time, work, and the papers they shared. Tiziana Casciaro's guidance, review of my early work, and support were hugely beneficial. I also wish to thank Tom Geraghty for his outstanding contribution to the body of work. I liken Tom's newsletter to the backbone and spinal cord of psychological safety. Also, it has been a pleasure learning with and from fellow Page Two coauthors Dr. Karolin Helbig and Minette Norman, who wrote *The Psychological Safety Playbook*. Finally, a brief conversation with Sue Barlow early on in my process helped spark the iterated title of this book. Thank you for speaking up, Sue!

I am very aware that my years spent on Simon Sinek's team have significantly helped me get to where I am in my life and career. I joined Simon's team as a young, eager, impatient, and naive twenty-four-year-old. I am beyond grateful for all I have learned, the opportunity provided to grow, and all the people I've been able to call colleagues, friends, and brothers and sisters over the many years.

My involvement with Simon's team introduced me to Ret. US Navy SEAL Commander Rich Diviney and his brilliant work, which I notably featured throughout this book. A huge thank-you to Rich and his wife and business partner, Kristen, for their unparalleled support, friendship, mentorship, and partnership.

Finally, I'd be remiss if I didn't thank and acknowledge my family and where I come from. I feel very connected to my heritage, on all sides of my family, as a descendent of Holocaust survivors and immigrants to Canada from Eastern Europe post–World War I and II.

I distinctly remember sitting in my office cubicle one day months into my first corporate job, the same job where a thousand people were let go on my first day. Feeling lost, dejected, and frustrated, I remember thinking about my grandfather, Benjamin, or Zaidie Ben. At my age then, twenty-three, my grandfather was on the Polish front line fighting with horses and rifles against the far superior, tank-drawn German army. After being captured, he spent two years in a prisoner of war camp near Berlin, hiding his Jewish identity. He escaped that prison, walked back home—at nighttime only—for six weeks straight, and married his childhood sweetheart, my grandmother, Eva. Upon returning home to his now Nazi-occupied small town, he said goodbye to much of his family for the last time. As his older and younger relatives were being sent off to work camps, Ben led a group of seven young adults into hiding for four years. By the end of the war, that group of seven had become five.

As I toiled in my first corporate job, I envisioned my grandfather and thought, with conviction, that I must do more. I was aware of how much my grandparents and ancestors went through to give my family and me a chance at a better life.

A couple years later, I chose to leave another corporate job in favor of my own entrepreneurial journey as a leadership development consultant, coach, and speaker. When I quit that *stable* corporate track, I got a phone call from Zaidie Ben, still a strong man at ninety-five years old. He demanded an explanation: "What are you doing, leaving a good job? Do you realize how much I sacrificed to give you and this family a better life?!" I explained to my grandfather, an entrepreneur himself (a butcher), that in his whole life, he had worked for someone else for only about six months, when he first landed in Toronto in 1953. I told him that I was inspired by his example, and I was following in his footsteps. That shut him up real quick. "Fine. Just don't sell drugs," he said.

I am happy to report that I have fulfilled that obligation. When Zaidie Ben passed away in August 2016, at the age of ninety-eight and eleven months, I vowed to live my life as a legacy to his. I hope and trust he has forgiven me for going the road less traveled.

I am surrounded by the most amazing family—parents, in-laws, siblings, aunts, uncles, cousins, and friends. I was able to bring this book to life because of them.

Notes

What's at Stake?

p. 1   *A passenger airplane dropped:* "Lion Air Crash: Indonesian Fishermen Recall How Plane Fell Out of Clear Sky and Crashed into Sea with Deafening Sound," *Straits Times*, October 30, 2018, straitstimes.com/ asia/se-asia/lion-air-crash-indonesian-fishermen-recall-how-plane-fell -out-of-clear-sky-and-crashed.

p. 1   *The pilots attempted to adjust:* Peter Robison, *Flying Blind: The 737 MAX Tragedy and the Fall of Boeing* (New York: Doubleday, 2021), 6.

p. 2   *every one and a half seconds, a Boeing 737 takes off:* Flight/Risk, official trailer, Prime Video, YouTube video, September 6, 2022, 2:35, youtu.be/ urYOTavhz6c.

p. 2   *The 737 MAX was Boeing's latest iteration:* Lewis Kamb, "Experts Question Whether Boeing's Board of Directors Is Capable of Righting the Company," *Seattle Times*, February 8, 2020, seattletimes.com/ business/boeing-aerospace/experts-question-whether-boeings-board -of-directors-is-capable-of-righting-the-company.

p. 2   *It served as a significant upgrade:* Robison, *Flying Blind*, 2.

p. 2   *the record climb of its stock price:* See the Boeing Co (BA) financial summary, Investing.com, investing.com/equities/boeing-co -financial-summary.

p. 2   *a combination of errors and leadership oversights:* Dan Pontefract, "Boeing's 737 MAX Crisis Is a Leadership Issue," *Forbes*, March 18, 2019, forbes.com/sites/danpontefract/2019/03/18/boeings-737-max -crisis-is-a-leadership-issue.

p. 2   *Much larger engines:* Joseph Herkert, Jason Borenstein, and Keith Miller, "The Boeing 737 MAX: Lessons for Engineering Ethics," *Science and Engineering Ethics* 26 (2020): 2957–74, doi.org/10.1007/s11948 -020-00252-y.

p. 3   *This meant it had a single point of failure:* All 737 MAX 8 airplanes now have two angle-of-attack sensors connected and sending information to the MCAS. They built in a backup to this safety-critical instrument, so it wasn't a single point of failure. Pilots are now also required to conduct full flight simulator training: See US Department of Transportation, Federal Aviation Administration, "Boeing 737-8 and 737-9 Airplanes: Pilot Training," N 8900.569, November 18, 2020, faa.gov/documentLibrary/media/Notice/N_8900.569_FAA_Web.pdf.

p. 3   *The MCAS essentially overrode:* Robison, *Flying Blind*, 7.

p. 3   *Boeing chalked the crash up:* Patrice Taddonio, "In 737 MAX Crashes, Boeing Pointed to Pilot Error—Despite a Fatal Design Flaw," PBS *Frontline*, September 14, 2021, pbs.org/wgbh/frontline/article/video -clip-boeing-737-max-crashes-fatal-design-flaw-documentary.

p. 3   *An even greater and wicked irony:* Will Horton, "Boeing Persuaded Lion Air to Forgo Simulator Training for 737 Max Pilots, Newly Released Messages Show," *Forbes*, January 10, 2020, forbes.com/ sites/willhorton1/2020/01/10/boeing-persuaded-lion-air-to-forgo -simulator-training-for-737-max-pilots.

p. 3   *former Boeing CEO Dennis Muilenburg shared:* Quoted in Peter Robison, "Boeing Built an Unsafe Plane, and Blamed the Pilots When It Crashed," *Bloomberg Businessweek*, November 16, 2021, bloomberg.com/news/ features/2021-11-16/are-boeing-planes-unsafe-pilots-blamed-for -corporate-errors-in-max-737-crash.

p. 3   *mentioned only once by name:* Mark Gollom, Alex Shprintsen, Frédéric Zalac, "737 Max Flight Manual May Have Left MCAS on 'Cutting Room Floor,'" CBC News, March 26, 2019, cbc.ca/news/ business/boeing-737-manual-mcas-system-plane-crash-1.5065842.

p. 3   *One Boeing employee, among others:* "Why Ed Pierson Won't Fly on a Boeing 737 MAX," *Corporate Crime Reporter*, January 24, 2022, corporatecrimereporter.com/news/200/why-ed-pierson-will-not-fly -on-a-boeing-737-max.

p. 5   *Ed Pierson, a retired US naval officer:* See Pierson's LinkedIn profile at linkedin.com/in/ed-pierson-a8b4b91ab.

p. 5   *In his final role with the company:* C-Span, "Former Boeing Employee Tells Lawmakers of Efforts to Warn about 737 Max Problems," video clip of "Boeing 737 MAX Aircraft Safety," December 11, 2019, 6:36, c-span.org/video/?c4838020/boeing-employee-tells-lawmakers -efforts-warn-737-max-problems.

p. 5   *With orders pouring in:* Ed Pierson, "Introduction," *Warning Bells with Ed Pierson*, podcast, episode 1, October 6, 2022, 14:25, edpierson.com/podcast.

p. 5   *Some employees reported:* Adam Grant, "Is It Safe to Speak Up at Work?" *WorkLife with Adam Grant*, podcast, season 4, episode 14, July 20, 2021, 37:00, ted.com/podcasts/worklife/is-it-safe-to-speak-up-at-work -transcript.

p. 5   *Fearing for the safety of:* Alexandra Ma, "A Boeing Whistleblower Says He Tried to Raise Concerns about Sloppy 737 MAX Production, but Was Ignored by the CEO, Board, FAA, and NTSB," *Business Insider*, December 10, 2019, businessinsider.com/boeing-737-max -whistleblower-ed-pierson-ceo-faa-ntsb-ignored-2019-12.

p. 5   *Pierson wrote in an email:* Grant, "Is It Safe to Speak Up at Work?"

p. 6   *Pierson pushed back:* "Why Ed Pierson Won't Fly."

p. 6   *In the* Corporate Crime Reporter: "Why Ed Pierson Won't Fly."

p. 6   *Although Pierson intended to work at Boeing:* "Why Ed Pierson Won't Fly."

p. 6   *an assistant high school football coach:* "Why Ed Pierson Won't Fly."

p. 6   *Over the next three months:* See Pierson's website, under Timeline, edpierson.com/timeline.

p. 7   *It too declined to act:* Cynthia McFadden, Anna Schecter, Kevin Monahan, and Rich Schapiro, "Former Boeing Manager Says He Warned Company of Problems Prior to 737 Crashes," NBC News, December 9, 2019, nbcnews.com/news/us-news/former-boeing-manager-says-he -warned-company-problems-prior-737-n1098536.

Chapter 1: How Did This Happen?

p. 9   *our relationship with our boss:* "Podcast: Dr. Casey Chosewood and Total Worker Health," *Truly Human Leadership Podcast* (formerly *Everybody Matters*), hosted by Brent Stewart, September 4, 2020, 44:15, barrywehmiller.com/post/podcast/2020/11/25/podcast-dr. -casey-chosewood-and-total-worker-health.

p. 10 *Muilenburg was known as:* Jeffrey Sonnenfeld, "Dennis Muilenburg's Moment," *Chief Executive*, n.d., chiefexecutive.net/dennis-muilenburgs -moment-of-crisis.

p. 11 *If you need proof:* Interaction Associates, *Building Workplace Trust: Trends and High Performance 2014/15*, report: 4, pdf4pro.com/cdn/ building-workplace-trust-interaction-29e61.pdf.

p. 12 *This passage tells the story:* See Luke 10:29–37, New International Version, Bible Gateway, biblegateway.com/passage/?search=Luke%20 10%3A29-37&version=NIV.

p. 13 *In the early 1970s, social psychologists:* John M. Darley and C. Daniel Batson, "'From Jerusalem to Jericho': A Study of Situational and Dispositional Variables in Helping Behavior," *Journal of Personality and*

Social Psychology 27, no. 1 (1973): 100–8, greatergood.berkeley.edu/
images/uploads/Darley-JersualemJericho.pdf.

p. 14   *Some of the participants who didn't stop:* Darley and Batson.

p. 14   *Safety and ethics evidently fell:* Caroline Adams Miller, "The Deadly
Mistake Many Companies Make with Their Goals," Medium, December
13, 2019, medium.com/@caroline_41467/goals-that-kill-how-heeding
-goal-setting-theory-could-have-helped-to-prevent-the-737-max
-disaster-40f5933b829c.

p. 14   *big purchasers like Southwest Airlines:* Michael Doran, "Did Southwest
Ask for a Modification to a 737 MAX to Deceive the FAA?" *Simple Flying,*
May 22, 2022, simpleflying.com/southwest-737-max-faa-deceit.

p. 14   *Boeing leaders were making hurried decisions:* John Cassidy, "How
Boeing and the F.A.A. Created the 737 MAX Catastrophe," *New Yorker,*
September 17, 2020, newyorker.com/news/our-columnists/how-boeing
-and-the-faa-created-the-737-max-catastrophe.

p. 16   *Ethical fading occurs:* "Ethical Fading," McCombs School of Business,
Ethics Unwrapped, video, n.d., 5:15, ethicsunwrapped.utexas.edu/video/
ethical-fading.

p. 16   *It is a form of self-deception:* Brett Beasley, "Keep Ethics from 'Fading'
When You Face a Tough Decision," Notre Dame Deloitte Center for
Ethical Leadership, n.d., ethicalleadership.nd.edu/news/ethical-fading
-dont-let-ethics-fade-from-view.

p. 16   *Ethical fading is one reason:* Beasley.

p. 16   *Tenbrunsel described the dangers:* Beasley; Roy J. Harris, "Jury in
Pinto Crash Case: 'We Wanted Ford to Take Notice,'" *Washington Post,*
February 15, 1978, washingtonpost.com/archive/politics/1978/02/15/
jury-in-pinto-crash-case-we-wanted-ford-to-take-notice/996a9aa5
-8f48-4541-8553-19c63f666830.

p. 16   *It took seven years:* "Ford Pinto Fuel-Fed Fires," The Center for Auto
Safety, n.d., autosafety.org/ford-pinto-fuel-fed-fires.

p. 16   *It also cost the company:* Gail Baura, "1978: Ford Pinto Recall," in
Engineering Ethics: An Industrial Perspective (Cambridge, MA:
Academic Press, 2006), 39–52; also Harris, "Jury in Pinto Crash Case."

p. 16   *Tenbrunsel and Messick explain:* Beasley, "Keep Ethics from Fading."

p. 19   *In the wake of the 2018 school shooting:* Rachel Siegel, "Dick's Sporting
Goods Overhauled Its Policies After Parkland. The CEO Didn't Stop
There," *Washington Post,* May 31, 2019, washingtonpost.com/business/
economy/dicks-sporting-goods-overhauled-its-gun-policies-after
-parkland-the-ceo-didnt-stop-there/2019/05/31/9faa6a08-7d8f-11e9
-a5b3-34f3edf1351e_story.html.

p. 19   *"We've just decided that:* David Caplan and Katie Kindelan, "Dick's
Sporting Goods CEO on Decision to No Longer Sell Assault-Style Rifles:
'We Don't Want to Be a Part of This Story,'" ABC News, February 28,
2018, abcnews.go.com/GMA/News/dicks-sporting-goods-ceo-company
-longer-sell-assault/story?id=53403284.

p. 19   *The choice drew outrage:* Caplan and Kindelan.

p. 19   *felt the financial impact:* Nathaniel Meyersohn, "Dick's Sporting
Goods Removes Guns and Ammo from 125 Stores," CNN Business,
March 14, 2019, cnn.com/2019/03/14/investing/dicks-sporting
-goods-guns/index.html.

p. 20   *In March 2019, DICK's announced:* Meyersohn.

p. 20   *And in March 2020:* Hannah Zhang, "Dick's Sporting Goods Will Stop
Selling Guns at 440 More Stores," CNN Business, March 10, 2020,
cnn.com/2020/03/10/business/dicks-sporting-goods-remove-guns
-from-440-stores/index.html.

p. 20   *Rather than lose revenue:* Zhang.

Chapter 2: Speaking Up Is Good for Business

p. 26   *Researchers at the Center for Talent Innovation:* Sylvia Ann
Hewlett, Melinda Marshall, and Laura Sherbin, with Tara Gonsalves,
Innovation, Diversity, and Market Growth, research report, Center
for Talent Innovation, September 2013, coqual.org/wp-content/
uploads/2020/09/31_innovationdiversityandmarketgrowth_
keyfindings-1.pdf.

p. 26   *They found that companies:* Sylvia Ann Hewlett, "Creating a Culture
Where Employees Speak Up," *Harvard Business Review,* January 8, 2016,
hbr.org/2016/01/creating-a-culture-where-employees-speak-up.

p. 27   *Mulally began his career:* "Alan Mulally," Corporate Executives, n.d.,
corporate-executives.com/executives/alan-mulally/.

p. 27   *He was largely credited with:* Michael Mecham and Anthony L. Velocci Jr.,
"Alan R. Mulally is AW&ST's Person of the Year," Aviation Week Network,
January 1, 2007, aviationweek.com/alan-r-mulally-awsts-person-year.

p. 27   *In the fifteen years before:* Simon Sinek, *The Infinite Game* (New York:
Portfolio/Penguin, 2019), 164.

p. 27   *At the formal press conference:* Viknesh Vijayenthiran, "New Ford CEO
Admits to Driving a Lexus LS," Motor Authority, September 11, 2006,
motorauthority.com/news/1029165_new-ford-ceo-admits-to-driving
-a-lexus-ls430.

p. 27   *After weeks of this charade:* Sinek, *Infinite Game,* 120.

p. 29   *Nadella also expects that leaders:* Satya Nadella, "The Meaning of Manager," in *Management Excellence at Microsoft: Model, Coach, Care,* LinkedIn Learning course, video, n.d., 1:20, linkedin.com/learning/ management-excellence-at-microsoft-model-coach-care/the -meaning-of-manager-14492917.

p. 29   *The Master of Demon Valley:* You can find this text in *Thunder in the Sky: Secrets on the Acquisition and Exercise of Power,* trans. Thomas Cleary (Shambhala Publications Inc., 1993).

p. 30   *Their 14 Leadership Traits:* "QPME: History and Traditions of the United States Marine Corps: Ethics, Values, and Leadership Development," Marine Corps University Research Library, updated January 20, 2023, grc-usmcu.libguides.com/pme/qpme/marine-corps -ethics-values-leadership-development/qualities.

p. 30   *11 Marine Corps Leadership Principles:* "QPME."

p. 30   *A study led by Susan Sorenson:* Susan Sorenson, "How Employees' Strengths Make Your Company Stronger," Gallup Workplace, n.d., gallup .com/workplace/231605/employees-strengths-company-stronger.aspx.

p. 32   *She surveyed healthcare workers:* Amy C. Edmondson, "Learning from Mistakes Is Easier Said Than Done: Group and Organizational Influences on the Detection and Correction of Human Error," *Journal of Applied Behavioral Science* 32, no. 1 (July 2016), doi.org/10.1177/00218 86396321001.

p. 32   *She defines psychological safety:* Amy C. Edmondson, in "Tool: Foster Psychological Safety," *re:Work,* n.d., rework.withgoogle.com/guides/ understanding-team-effectiveness/steps/foster-psychological-safety.

p. 33   *That meant worse outcomes:* Adam Grant, *Think Again: The Power of Knowing What You Don't Know* (New York: Viking, 2021).

p. 33   *The late psychologist:* Richard Farson and Ralph Keyes, "The Failure-Tolerant Leader," *Harvard Business Review,* August 2002, hbr.org/ 2002/08/the-failure-tolerant-leader.

p. 34   *"The fastest way to succeed:* Quoted in Farson and Keyes.

p. 35   *L.D. DeSimone, former CEO of 3M:* Farson and Keyes.

Chapter 3: Speak Up, Why Don't You?

p. 38   *They dug into the two:* Hemant Kakkar and Subra Tangirala, "If Your Employees Aren't Speaking Up, Blame Company Culture," *Harvard Business Review,* November 6, 2018, hbr.org/2018/11/if-your -employees-arent-speaking-up-blame-company-culture.

p. 38   *both personality and situation influenced:* Kakkar and Tangirala.

p. 42   *group size significantly affects:* Gus Cooney, Adam M. Mastroianni, Nicole Abi-Esber, and Alison Wood Brooks, "The Many Minds Problem: Disclosure in Dyadic versus Group Conversation," *Current Opinions in Psychology* 31 (February 2020): 22–27, doi.org/10.1016/j.copsyc .2019.06.032.

p. 47   *This was also the case for:* BrainLine, "Coast Guard Veteran Kimberly Young-McLear, PhD on Saving Herself and Others by Being a Whistleblower," YouTube video, February 10, 2023, 3:14, youtu.be/n2fx3xjbyUw.

p. 48   *deciding whether to speak up:* Elizabeth J. McClean, Sean R. Martin, Kyle J. Emich, and Col. Todd Woodruff, "The Social Consequences of Voice: An Examination of Voice Type and Gender on Status and Subsequent Leader Emergence," *Academy of Management Journal* 61, no. 5 (October 24, 2018), doi.org/10.5465/amj.2016.0148.

p. 48   *A "gaslighter" uses four main techniques:* "Types of Gaslighting," Studious Guy, n.d., studiousguy.com/types-of-gaslighting.

p. 51   *a record number of people quit their jobs:* "Interactive Chart: How Historic Has the Great Resignation Been?" SHRM, March 9, 2022, shrm.org/resourcesandtools/hr-topics/talent-acquisition/pages/ interactive-quits-level-by-year.aspx.

p. 51   *According to Gallup:* Jim Harter, "U.S. Employee Engagement Data Holds Steady in First Half of 2021," Gallup Workplace, April 8, 2022, gallup.com/workplace/352949/employee-engagement-holds-steady -first-half-2021.aspx.

p. 51   *employers are losing out on:* Josh Fechter, "What Is the Cost of Disengaged Employees?" HR University, December 22, 2012, hr.university/analytics/cost-of-disengaged-employees.

p. 51   *That's equal to 11 percent:* Ryan Pendell, "The World's $7.8 Trillion Workplace Problem," Gallup Workplace, June 14, 2022, gallup.com/ workplace/393497/world-trillion-workplace-problem.aspx.

p. 52   *individuals must ask:* Liane Davey, "A Different Take on Psychological Safety," September 19, 2021, lianedavey.com/a-different-take-on -psychological-safety.

p. 52   *if they are fearful that:* Davey.

Chapter 4: Leadership Defined

p. 60   *during his military career:* Rich Diviney, *The Attributes: 25 Hidden Drivers of Optimal Performance* (New York: Random House, 2021), 197.

p. 61   *"All types of leaders:* Diviney.

p. 61   *"Leaders aren't born:* Diviney.

p. 64   *He identifies those as:* Diviney.

p. 69   *the power leaders inherit:* Jerry Useem, "Power Causes Brain Damage," *The Atlantic,* July/August 2017, theatlantic.com/magazine/archive/ 2017/07/power-causes-brain-damage/528711.

p. 70   *As when Michelle Obama:* Anne Applebaum, "Michelle Obama: Is First Ladies' Club Ready?" AEI, July 12, 2008, aei.org/articles/ michelle-obama-is-first-ladies-club-ready.

Chapter 5: Select Better Leaders

p. 77   *Frans de Waal studies:* Frans de Waal, "The Surprising Science of Alpha Males," TEDMed 2017, video, 15:46, ted.com/talks/frans_de_waal_ the_surprising_science_of_alpha_males.

p. 78   *Diviney shares a story:* Rich Diviney, *The Attributes: 25 Hidden Drivers of Optimal Performance* (New York: Random House, 2021), 224.

Chapter 6: Help Leaders Lead

p. 91   *"Practicing anything mildly important:* Jack Zenger, "We Wait Too Long to Train Our Leaders," *Harvard Business Review,* December 17, 2012, hbr.org/2012/12/why-do-we-wait-so-long-to-trai.

p. 92   *"Supervisors are, of course:* Zenger.

p. 92   *"With all the money and effort:* Zenger.

p. 96   *The 5 Languages of Appreciation are:* Gary Chapman and Paul White, *The 5 Languages of Appreciation in the Workplace: Empowering Organizations by Encouraging People* (New York: Northfield Publishing, 2019).

Chapter 7: Culture Matters

p. 107   *announcement from the Business Roundtable:* Michael Hiltzik, "Column: Last Year CEOs Pledged to Serve Stakeholders, Not Shareholders. You Were Right Not to Buy It," from *Los Angeles Times,* August 19, 2020, *Yahoo!* Movies, ca.movies.yahoo.com/column-ago-ceos-pledged -serve-130028409.html.

p. 107   *A declaration, signed by 181 CEOs:* "Business Roundtable Redefines the Purpose of a Corporation to Promote 'An Economy That Serves All Americans,'" Business Roundtable, August 19, 2019, businessroundtable.org/business-roundtable-redefines-the-purpose -of-a-corporation-to-promote-an-economy-that-serves-all-americans.

p. 109   *"I felt it was incumbent on me:* Indra K. Nooyi, *My Life in Full: Work, Family, and Our Future* (New York: Portfolio, 2021), 201.

p. 109   *Finally, Ulukaya, often called:* Hamdi Ulukaya, "The Anti-CEO
         Playbook," TED2019, video, 19:09, ted.com/talks/hamdi_ulukaya_the_
         anti_ceo_playbook.

p. 109   *The profit-sharing model:* Mary Josephs, "What Does Chobani's
         Founder Get for Giving 10% of His Company to Workers?" *Forbes,*
         April 29, 2016, forbes.com/sites/maryjosephs/2016/04/29/what-does
         -chobanis-founder-get-for-giving-10-of-his-company-to-workers.

p. 109   *In less than five years:* Ulukaya, "The Anti-CEO Playbook."

p. 109   *In his brilliant book:* L. David Marquet, *Turn the Ship Around! A True
         Story of Turning Followers Into Leaders* (London, UK: Portfolio, 2015).

p. 110   *the Santa Fe also produced:* "Captain David Marquet, Captain of USS
         Santa Fe—Inspiring Leadership Interview with Jonathan Bowman-Perks
         MBE," *Inspiring Leadership Podcast,* episode 120, January 2, 2021,
         46:45, jonathanperks.com/podcasts/captain-david-marquet-captain-of
         -uss-santa-fe-inspiring-leadership-interview-with-jonathan-bowman
         -perks-mbe.

p. 111   *He calls this "self-perception theory":* "Self-Perception Theory," Learning
         Theories, n.d., learning-theories.com/self-perception-theory-bem.html.

p. 113   *As human beings, we aren't designed:* R.I.M. Dunbar, "Neocortex Size as
         a Constraint on Group Size in Primates," *Journal of Human Evolution* 22,
         no. 6 (1992): 469–93, doi.org/10.1016/0047-2484(92)90081-J.

p. 119   *a study on leadership communication:* Adam Grant (@AdamMGrant),
         "Repeat after me: good communication requires repetition," Twitter,
         August 25, 2022, 11:07 a.m., twitter.com/AdamMGrant/status/
         1562818994926628864; Francis J. Flynn and Chelsea R. Lide,
         "Communication Miscalibration: The Price Leaders Pay for Not
         Sharing Enough," *Academy of Management Journal* (July 25, 2022),
         doi.org/10.5465/amj.2021.0245.

p. 122   *the avoidance of hard conversations:* Liane Davey, *The Good Fight: Use
         Productive Conflict to Get Your Team and Organization Back on Track*
         (Vancouver: Page Two, 2019), 7–26.

p. 124   *a person may fear an aversive outcome:* Liane Davey, "A Different Take
         on Psychological Safety," September 19, 2021, lianedavey.com/
         a-different-take-on-psychological-safety.

Chapter 8: The Virtuous Cycle of "Encourage and Reward"

p. 127   *These were words shared by:* Brené Brown with Scott Sonenshein,
         "Why We'll Never Be the Same Again (and Why It's Time to Talk About It),"
         Dare to Lead, podcast, April 11, 2022, 55:33, brenebrown.com/podcast/
         why-well-never-be-the-same-again-and-why-its-time-to-talk-about-it.

p. 128 *just because there are fewer errors reported:* Amy C. Edmondson, "Learning from Mistakes Is Easier Said Than Done: Group and Organizational Influences on the Detection and Correction of Human Error," *Journal of Applied Behavioral Science* 32, no. 1 (March 1996), doi.org/10.1177/0021886396321001.

p. 136 *"The basic human challenge is this:* Amy Edmondson, "Leading by Learning with Amy Edmondson," *World Reimagined,* podcast, season 3, episode 7, July 12, 2022, 33:15, nasdaq.com/podcast/leading-by -learning-with-amy-edmondson.

p. 136 *his father, who was a tribal chief and community leader:* Malky McEwan, "3 Valuable Lessons Nelson Mandela Learned from His Father," *Medium,* October 24, 2021, medium.com/better-advice/three-valuable-lessons -nelson-mandela-learned-from-his-father-3e3f0e850834.

p. 137 *In an interview, Edmondson describes:* Edmondson.

p. 138 *Adam Grant suggests making things quantitative:* Adam Grant (@AdamMGrant), "When people hesitate to give honest feedback on an idea, draft, or performance, I ask for a 0–10 score . . ." Twitter, August 25, 2022, 2:30 p.m., twitter.com/AdamMGrant/ status/1369732419021135879.

p. 138 *74 percent of employees: State of Employee Feedback 2021,* AllVoices, May 14, 2021, allvoices.co/blog/state-of-employee-feedback-2021.

p. 139 *The same report found that: State of Employee Feedback 2021.*

Chapter 9: Feedback Is a Dish Best Shared

p. 147 *a concept I've adopted from:* Kim Scott, *Radical Candor: Be a Kick-Ass Boss without Losing Your Humanity* (New York: St. Martin's, 2017).

p. 160 *article shared survey results:* Jack Zenger and Joseph Folkman, "Why Do So Many Managers Avoid Giving Praise?" *Harvard Business Review,* May 2, 2017, hbr.org/2017/05/why-do-so-many-managers -avoid-giving-praise.

Chapter 10: What's Really at Stake?

p. 164 *One was a first-generation immigrant: List(e)n,* directed by Juliana Tafur (Story Powerhouse and Orkidea Films, 2020), listencourageously.com/ thefilm.

p. 166 *One company, Basecamp:* Megan Reitz and John Higgins, "Don't Ban 'Politics' at Work," *Harvard Business Review,* July 7, 2021, hbr.org/ 2021/07/dont-ban-politics-at-work.

p. 167 *This was the case for Nate Swann:* Stephen "Shed" Shedletzky, "Incorporating Neurodiversity with Hiren Shukla and Nate Swann," YouTube video, April 14, 2022, 1:04:21, youtu.be/vtOu5-ajdcA.

p. 169   *That kind of thinking inspired Shukla:* Shedletzky.

p. 171   *Importantly, Shukla says:* Shedletzky.

p. 171   *stand-up comedy bit from 1992:* "George Carlin: Saving the Planet—Transcript," from *George Carlin: Jamming In New York* (1992), Scraps from the Loft, August 22, 2019, scrapsfromtheloft.com/comedy/george-carlin-saving-planet-transcript.

p. 174   *"We can disagree and still love each other:* This quote is often misattributed to author James Baldwin. In fact, author and activist Robert Jones Jr., who calls himself "Son of Baldwin," tweeted these words. You can read more on that here: galeriadelaraza.org/eng/events/index.php?op=view&id=6704.

p. 174   *"Empathy fuels connection:* RSA, "Brené Brown on Empathy," YouTube video, December 10, 2013, 2:53, youtu.be/1Evwgu369Jw.

p. 174   *Meanwhile, sympathy is when:* RSA.

p. 175   *After she spent considerable time:* White Right: Meeting the Enemy, directed by Deeyah Khan (Fuuse Films, 2017), deeyah.com/blog/white-right-meeting-enemy.

p. 176   *"Between stimulus and response:* This quotation is often misattributed to Viktor Frankl and others. Quote Investigator, however, writes: "In 1994 [Stephen] Covey co-authored a book titled 'First Things First' with A. Roger Merrill, and Rebecca R. Merrill. In this work Covey presented an exact match to the quotation under examination. He saw the words in an unnamed book, but he employed the phrase 'the essence of it' to signal that his memory was inexact: Stephen: Years ago, as I was wandering between the stacks of books at a university library, I chanced to open a book in which I encountered one of the most powerful, significant ideas I've ever come across. The essence of it was this:

Between stimulus and response, there is a space.
In that space is our power to choose our response.
In our response lies our growth and our freedom.

That idea hit me with incredible force. In the following days, I reflected on it again and again.'"

For more, see quoteinvestigator.com/2018/02/18/response.

Chapter 11: It's Personal

p. 185   *Its impact is on par with:* Tracy Brower, "Managers Have Major Impact on Mental Health: How to Lead for Wellbeing," *Forbes*, January 29, 2023, forbes.com/sites/tracybrower/2023/01/29/managers-have-major-impact-on-mental-health-how-to-lead-for-wellbeing.

Index

About the Author

STEPHEN SHEDLETZKY—or "Shed" to his friends—helps leaders make it safe and worth it for people to speak up. He supports humble leaders—those who know they are part of both the problems they experience and the solutions they can create—as they put their people and purpose first.

A sought-after speaker, coach, and advisor, Shed has led hundreds of keynote presentations, workshops, and leadership development programs. As a thought leader on psychological safety in the workplace and creating speak-up cultures where people and organizations thrive, he works with leaders around the world and serves clients in all industries where human beings work.

He graduated from the Ivey Business School with a focus on leadership, communication, and strategy, and received his coaching certification from the Co-Active Training Institute. Shed lives in Toronto, Canada, with his wife and two children.

Want to Do More to Nurture a Speak-Up Culture?

Let's do it.

Contact team@shedinspires.com to inquire about

- keynotes and fireside chats,
- workshops and trainings,
- executive coaching,
- advising,
- speak-up culture assessments, and
- bulk orders and book clubs for your team, community, or organization.

- SpeakUpCulture.com
- linkedin.com/in/stephenshedletzky
- @shedinspires
- #SpeakUpCulture